ARCHITECT

+

ENTREPRENEUR

A Field Guide to

Building, Branding, and Marketing

Your Startup Design Business

Eric W. Reinholdt
[thirtybyforty.com]
Mount Desert Island, Maine

All rights reserved. No part of this publication may be reproduced, distributed, or transmitted in any form or by any means, including photocopying, recording, or other electronic or mechanical methods, without the prior written permission of the publisher, except in the case of brief quotations embodied in critical reviews and certain other noncommercial uses permitted by copyright law. For permission requests, please contact the author at the address below.

30X40 Design Workshop
12 Brendun Lane
Mount Desert, Maine 04660
http://thirtybyforty.com

DISCLAIMER

Although the author has made every effort to ensure that the information in this book was correct at press time, the author does not assume and hereby disclaim any liability to any party for any loss, damage, or disruption caused by errors or omissions, whether such errors or omissions result from negligence, accident, or any other cause. The author does not represent, warrant, undertake or guarantee: that the information in the book is correct, accurate, or complete; or that the use of the guidance in the book will lead to any particular outcome or result. The author of this book is not affiliated with any official source for the subjects of this book. The author does not represent any company mentioned in the text or its affiliates and no infringement of trademark is intended.

Copyright © 2015 by Eric W. Reinholdt

I hope this book inspires you to begin
building your design business - today.

If you have questions or need
help, feel free to get in touch.

Cheers,
Eric Reinholdt
http://thirtybyforty.com

30X40
DESIGN.WORKSHOP

Download the tools and resources I use to run 30X40 Design Workshop in the A+E Startup Toolkit (Volume 1) located here: http://thirtybyforty.com/spl

Additional resources created exclusively for readers, can be found at: **http://thirtybyforty.com/sign-up**

TABLE OF CONTENTS

Introduction _____ 6

1 | Mindset _____ 10

2 | Getting Started _____ 22

3 | Your Brand _____ 42

4 | Marketing _____ 51

5 | Internet Marketing _____ 67

6 | Getting Hired _____ 82

7 | Getting Paid (Your Contract) _____ 105

8 | Finances _____ 118

9 | Studio Essentials _____ 129

10 | Startup Costs _____ 140

11 | SOP's _____ 152

12 | Software _____ 160

Closing Thoughts + Resources _____ 170

Introduction

"Think big, start small, learn fast." – Eric Ries

Opening my business has been the best career decision of my life. I've written this book as the handbook I was seeking when I transitioned from employee to founder. I hope it inspires you to create your own path.

Before opening 30X40 Design Workshop, I was searching for a recipe for starting an architecture business. I wanted specifics, a checklist, a step-by-step instruction guide to parcel out the monumental into the manageable. I wanted a framework that I could pick up when I had free time - in the early mornings, during my lunch break, and in the evenings.

But I couldn't find one.

The AIA (American Institute of Architects) publications were uninspired and outdated. The Handbook for Professional Practice and Architect's Essentials of Starting a Design Firm each read like contracts. They were primarily written for those intending to build colossal firms, not a sole proprietor building a small business in the 21st century. I found myself laughing at some of the antiquated advice about marketing and software, including a recommendation for PaintShop Pro? Really?

I had questions, probably the same questions you have. I wanted to understand how to interview, what kind of website to build, what software I needed, how to structure my contract and how to get paid. What were the real-world business situations I would face?

If you've been searching for similar practical information, this book is your field guide.

My career in architecture has followed the well-worn path of many architects before me; from professional degree to internship to licensure and on to practice. I graduated with a Bachelor of Architecture in 1996 and pursued design work, at varying scales, throughout New England – schools, health care facilities, civic institutions and private homes. Most of my working life was spent in a conventional 8am – 5pm (quite often much later) studio environment.

I commuted an hour each way, every day and with every job I held. I completed time sheets accounting for my every sixth minute (1/10th of an hour) of billable time. I had always worked for someone else and was rewarded for my loyalty every two weeks with a paycheck. It felt like a stable existence.

Still, I longed for something different. I wanted my own practice. But that was an idea reserved for an indeterminate time far in the future, a time when there was plenty of work and when I was ready. I treated this idea as sacred, it was one that I kept like a trophy on a shelf, where I could pick it up and dust it off occasionally. Every time I entertained the thought that part inside me that's wired for survival and protection -- what Seth Godin calls the 'Lizard Brain' -- protested and logically advised me not to.

I found that discussing the idea with friends or family was far easier than the thought of actually executing and delivering on the promise. Discussing it, in a way, felt as if I had already done it. Announcing it to others without any sort of accountability satisfied the desire without demanding action.

> "I'd like to have more work lined up before I make a go of it. Probably next year," I would say.

Of course, the next year would arrive, my salary would be slightly higher, my children would be one year closer to college and I'd be committed to another design project in the office that I'd want to see finished.

Does this sound familiar? Are you this architect or designer?

In early 2013, on the cusp of turning forty, my dream job designing high-end homes on the coast of Maine was facing uncertain times.

My employer had cut our salaries by 20% and gave us the choice of working for no pay on Fridays or pursuing outside work on our own. I once again picked up that precious trophy, dusted it off, listened to the protests of my lizard brain and this time, I ignored them. I knew this was my chance to get started building something I could call my own and a business capable of supporting my family.

The process of designing architecture, working with clients and building buildings, that was familiar territory. I knew I could do the work, but at the time I knew next to nothing about operating a business. So I read. I began with the AIA (American Institute of Architects) "Architect's Essentials" and "The Handbook for Professional Practice." But they seemed to describe a historic past. I was looking for a handbook, a step-by-step guide, something I could reference when I had a question.

I turned to online resources, blogs, forums and articles and found a group of young professionals grappling with the same problems. The information I discovered there was timely and based on real experiences. These were individuals designing practices like I was – from nothing – and succeeding. I read case studies, listened to podcasts, corresponded with pros who made the leap before me, studied business plans, made lists, sketched out weighted average decision matrices, pondered, and researched some more. Every time I found new information I felt as though I had just scraped the surface of what was available. I had so much more to learn.

Research paralysis is common; it's also a subconscious delay tactic. It keeps us safely in the harbor when we need to be fishing. Reading and researching about how to open a design practice is a necessary part of the process. Following others who have built successful businesses too. But as I look back, I can tell you that there's just no substitute for that important first leap. Reading about it can be reassuring, but stepping out is **required**. One can't possibly know all the questions one needs to ask when sitting in the relative comfort of a salaried job.

The experience of sole practice has taught me what no amount of research ever could have. The truth is there's nothing you can do to escape the labor in front of you when you set out on your own. Building a business is hard work. You're investing in an unknown asset, giving it form; shaping it from nothing. Crafting a brand and a business to support you will probably count among the most difficult things you've done in your life; it will also be one of the most rewarding.

Opening your own practice offers more job security than any other job could ever provide. This might seem counterintuitive, but remember your current job is subject to change at any moment. If your employer told you that your salary has been reduced by 20% effective tomorrow, would you have any say? When you work for someone else they control your time and your future, what type of work you'll do, and what you'll be paid in exchange for that work. Your own business, by contrast, is something no one can ever take from you. It's yours, you own it, and you chart the course.

It comes at a cost though; hard work, persistence, and much anxiety. In the early stages accepting these as part of doing business will be challenging. You'll be excited to begin designing, everything will be new and shiny and as your excitement is peaking no one else will be listening (except your close friends and family).

I've written this book as a catalyst for you to take the actions necessary to open your own design practice. It isn't a singular vision of how to do it though. There are many ways to practice your craft today; begin to think like an entrepreneur and you'll see opportunity everywhere. This book will instill in you the confidence that it's possible to build a life and practice that rewards your individual talents and skills. If you choose, it can be a life that doesn't trade time or hours worked for dollars.

The text is designed to remove the barriers you'll encounter along the way and answer the basic questions all business owners face because I know that even simple barriers can be cleverly used as an excuse - a red light - for not progressing. Opening your design practice doesn't require all the lights to be green.

It all starts with action.

1 | Mindset

*"If you really want to do something, you'll find a way.
If you don't, you'll find an excuse."– Jim Rohn*

Have you ever tried to brew your own beer? If you have, you know that homebrewing is a unique combination of cooking, drinking, and science. I decided I wanted to give it a try and so I purchased a starter kit, found a recipe for a pale ale and purchased the ingredients – hops, yeast, and grain. What could be more satisfying than freshly brewed homemade ale? As I read the recipe, each step sounded simple, but the sum total – the entire process – wasn't at all.

The questions started to mount: How long should I mash the grains? At what temperature? The airlock isn't bubbling? Is the fermentation stuck? Do I have enough yeast to naturally carbonate? Is the water hot enough; is it too soft or too hard? How do I keep things from boiling over? There were grains to crack, wort to boil, hops to add, yeast to pitch, finished beer to bottle. And finally - three weeks later - fresh ale to drink.

In the end, the beer came out fine. Not great, just fine. With some practice I could've made it better, probably much better. But I learned that just because I like ale, it doesn't mean I need make it myself. I don't need to own a microbrewery.

Starting your own design practice is like this too. As is often the case, many simple steps taken together coalesce into a great deal of work. Do you need to own the firm to enjoy practicing architecture or interior design? Maybe not.

To determine whether you're mentally ready for the work ahead, establishing the proper mindset is your first task.

CEO and Architect. Deciding to open your own design practice requires a fundamental shift in attitude toward the making of architecture. You're a business owner first. To survive in the long-term a business' expenses must be lower than their income. It's that simple. You must prioritize learning to be a businessperson over being an architect. This is especially crucial when you're staking your claim and building your reputation.

This isn't to say that everything you love about architecture has to be packed up and traded away when you assume the role as CEO of your business. It just means that design will have a different place in your operations and occasionally, it may even defer to your business decisions.

Not long after opening my practice I was approached by a potential client. Like me, he had a young family, he wanted a small home and of course he had an even smaller budget. I could relate to his position, I had been in that exact spot a few years earlier. I remember looking at the existing (extremely expensive) housing stock and feeling disheartened.

I wanted to help him design his home; it was an interesting project and small is what I do well. But it quickly became clear that he was interviewing many architects (more than six is a sure sign of indecisiveness) for a chance at an extremely small fee (a sign of unrealistic expectations). I quoted him a price before agreeing to step into the pool of interviewees. I proposed a fee that would've allowed me to remain profitable and I suggested that given his budget he needed me even more.

I never heard from him again. Just because I love designing small homes doesn't mean I can do it for free and small projects with small budgets are just as much, if not more work than the larger ones. In that situation I prioritized business over design and I'm glad I did, because it left room on my boards for the next project, one more aligned with the value that I offer.

And there's always a next project.

I won't always accept jobs based on profitability but I want the flexibility to be selective. Imagine if every project you accepted had a razor thin margin of profitability. It's the worst possible position to be in, always behind, always struggling, with no room for error. Prioritizing profitability builds in flexibility to your operations. It allows you to carefully consider and accept only those unprofitable projects that have the most impact -- in your community, in your business -- wherever you decide.

This is the kind of mindset you'll have to adopt if you're to take seriously the step of starting your design practice.

Amateur versus Professional. I started my business moonlighting while working at another firm. Like many other architects, I treated this work more as a hobby than a business. I was a professional treating my side work as an amateur and consequently, there was very little financially at stake. If a client put a project on hold indefinitely it only meant that some of my discretionary income went down; it didn't mean I couldn't afford my utility bill.

I didn't run P+L reports; I didn't have to take a client meeting on a Saturday if I didn't want to. If the work came to me I would gladly do it, but I wasn't planning to build something larger. Extra cash in my pocket was nice but there wasn't any pressure to actively market myself or create a repetitive formula for success.

There's an important distinction between practicing your craft as an amateur and doing it as a professional.

Because there's nothing at stake, the amateur isn't committed to long-term success, only short-term gains. Professionals are invested in success and have a long-term plan for making it happen. Perhaps most importantly, the professional realizes that every action has real, legal implications. It's an intimidating thought but your professional reputation is built on the each one of these actions.

When you're an amateur, the grey areas of practice will consistently challenge you. The amateur treats earnings from a moonlighting job as "spending money" ignoring the quarterly tax due. Clients will ask that you look the other way and ignore the building code offering, "no one will know."

Grey areas are for amateurs; the professional is unflinching and decisive in their commitment to always follow the rules. Which reputation would you prefer to have? You can't afford to do favors or look the other way; it's *your* professional reputation and *our* profession at stake. You have a legal professional obligation to uphold. It's one that you agreed to when you became a licensed professional. You have a duty to serve and protect the public. If you encounter situations where these things are required of you simply walk away.

Being a pro also requires committing the necessary time and effort to running your business professionally. There's a lot more to running a design practice than design. You'll probably spend fewer hours designing than ever before when you open your own business. There's marketing, invoicing, closing deals, clients to meet, contractors asking questions, consultants to coordinate, site visits, phone calls to take and make, e-mails to answer, and letters to write. These things take time and usually that's time taken away from design duties.

Unfortunately, assuming a professional role means that the time spent designing architecture is more limited. If you're the kind of person who needs large doses of daily design time, opening your own business isn't the best way to get your fix. You're probably better off working as an employee in a firm that prioritizes design and can handle the myriad tasks that secure the projects you'll design.

You'll be busy running the business first: invoicing, marketing, paying bills, doing taxes, ordering office supplies, finishing the drawings for your current project, writing meeting notes.

Professional status carries with it a responsibility to represent all architects well. Serve your client's needs, orchestrate solutions, seek adequate compensation for the value you bring and do good work. You owe it to your colleagues to uphold the high standards of the profession. When you're working for someone else they carry that mantle – when you step out on your own, you carry it.

When you can commit to being a professional rather than an amateur, you're ready to tackle the next mindset problem.

Overcoming Fear of Failure. To be honest, facing my fear of failure was a larger hurdle than almost anything I've encountered in business. What I've come to accept is that it's all a matter of perception. One can either choose to acknowledge the fear, feel it and let it pass, or simply be paralyzed by it. It's an easy decision when you frame it like that right? You can't change the fact that you'll feel the fear, only how you react to it.

Here are a few tactics that helped me acknowledge, accept and move forward despite my fears.

1 - **Imagine the worst possible outcome.** The first step to making your business venture real is to actually allow yourself to imagine it. And, the most pressing question, the one that's keeping you from committing, is, "What if I fail?" You need to honestly answer the question. What if you fail? Write down the answer on a sheet of paper, make it real. If you leave your current job to make a run at this and it fails -- meaning no clients, no income, no one calling -- what then? Will you lose your home? Will you lose the respect of your peers, your family and your friends? Will you have lost your life savings to make your dream a reality? Define what's really at stake. There's an answer to each of these questions.

For me, after working through those questions, I arrived at the following worst-case conclusion: "I'll have to find another job". For you, it may be different. I found this worst-case conclusion to be somewhat circular; the worst case wasn't actually that bad. It was one I was already familiar with – a job working for someone else.

Ready for the bonus? You may even find a better job than you have now. When you learn to embrace the fear, accept it and let it go by logically thinking through the range of possible outcomes you own it, it doesn't own you.

2 – **Redefine success and failure.** What do they really mean? Are they monetary thresholds? Professional recognition? Family recognition? Spousal acceptance? Personal happiness? Something else? It's easy to adopt the definitions of these terms from our societal norms - the expensive car, the waterfront property, the boat, and exotic vacations. Would having these define success or not having them define failure for you?

When pressed, most of us would define success very simply: to control how we spend our time, to be mentally fulfilled, and to feel necessary. These all contribute to our happiness and are the real feelings underlying our definitions of success. Too often the definition of success or failure replaces these emotional values with forthright expressions of wealth because that's what we've been acculturated to, not because they're what really matter to us.

You're probably afraid to fail because you won't be seen as successful. But consider whether your current job is meeting your definition of success. If you're unhappy then you've already failed. You've already been there. You know what it feels like. Is your family judging you for this? Probably not. Are your friends? Other professionals?

If you accept that you've already failed, then the choice to try again is an easy one. Perhaps you should be more afraid of not trying than trying and failing.

Articulating your definition of success and establishing goals for your business and your personal life creates a reliable framework for the decisions you'll face along the way. When the road forks you'll choose the path that contributes to those goals and ultimately your definition of what it means to be successful.

Many perceive the act of opening a business as a singular act - one that they either pass or fail at. I believe this is a flawed perception - opening a business isn't a zero-sum game. You'll always walk away with more than you started with - more knowledge, a better understanding of the world, more connections, and a dose of pride that you actually tried and didn't let the dream languish in a perpetual state of, "Yes, I plan to open my practice one day, but the time isn't quite right."

You can always earn another dollar, but you'll never earn another minute. Time is a finite resource; we only have a limited (and unknowable) amount of it to invest. Having control of my time and how I invest it is my ultimate definition of a successful life. I want to have the flexibility to explore and learn new things each day and control my own time. I've designed my business as an instrument to allow that to happen.

By opening your own business you're embracing the opportunity to shape your future. As an employee, you're building someone else's definition of success.

3 – **Just get started.** We're all guilty of research paralysis. There will always be another blog post or book to read, another case study to take notes on, another person's advice to solicit. But there's just no substitute for actually doing the work. Digging into a set of tasks, especially rote ones, will help quiet your internal anxieties and quell your fears. Busy your mind solving genuine business problems rather than prognosticating on failure. You can tick off the checkboxes of necessary business tasks from the (relative) safety of your current job. Along the way you'll formulate new questions; the things you didn't know that you didn't know.

Leverage the natural transition points that happen throughout your normal day – whether it's the early morning, evenings, on your commute (if possible) or during lunch. Find the time you focus best and dedicate it to starting your business.

I work best in the morning and so I used that time to lay the foundations of my business. You can too. There's no escaping the fact that starting your own business, aside from assuming great personal and professional responsibility, requires plenty of extra time and hours. Working consistently, day after day in your spare time not only gets you closer to the reality, but it establishes the kind of work habits you'll need to make your business succeed. You'll be amazed at the results consistently applied effort can yield.

These short snippets of focused time are good opportunities to flesh out branding and logo designs, your business card, content creation, writing, web design, and a time to develop your business standard operating procedures.

You can begin today, right now if you choose.

4 – **List the Pros and Cons.** It helps to rationally look at the positives and negatives and I like lists, so here's one I developed when I was contemplating the possibility of opening my practice. The parentheses indicate whether I think they're a net positive or negative. Your answers may differ.

Time (+) This is first on the list because it's the most important asset we have and it's the one thing you can never get more of. Using time for its highest and best purpose should be everyone's goal. At the end of your life you'll always want more. But, take today as an example and carefully look at the time you've wasted – commuting, reading BuzzFeed, checking e-mail – are you treating it like the precious resource it really is?

The first thing I noticed when I stopped working for someone else was the amount of time I spent commuting. A full two (or more depending on traffic) hours each day just moving my body back and forth between my home and an office. That's 10 hours a week, 500 hours a year! Think of what you could do with 500 hours of extra time. At $100 per hour (a conservative hourly rate) that's $50,000 of additional income (before taxes). But that's just a financial accounting of the value of time, it's impossible to put a price on being there to watch your children grow up or extra time with a spouse or your family.

Controlling your schedule, the things you work on, the people you work with, what projects you accept or reject –owning your time is a huge win. Starting your own business means you spend time on the things *you* think are most important.

Benefits (-) If you work in a place that provides fringe benefits, you'll suddenly realize how valuable (and expensive) they are.

You'll be responsible for saving for retirement, for health and life insurance yourself now. This is a personal decision that may be a pro or a con, either way it's a necessary one especially if you have a family.

Responsibility (+/-) Initially, the idea that you call all the shots is an invigorating feeling. But shouldering all of the responsibility, all of the time, is a lonely and thankless job. You make the coffee, you clean, you set the budget, develop the design concept, do the drafting, answer the phone, manage angry clients, do the invoicing, market the business, secure new work, show up for the interview, attend the public hearing, write the specifications and so on. To make the business a success it's all required, none of it can slip. There's nowhere for it slip to, everything stops with you.

There's no getting around the fact that owning a business is a lot of hard work. It's a lot for one person to handle. If the thought is too overwhelming, consider a partner who can complement your skill set and share in the responsibility of running the business.

Taxes (+/-) This can be a positive or a negative depending on a variety of factors, not the least of which being how much you actually earn. Rent, utilities, books, magazines, fees, advertising, supplies, printers, computers, and furniture – these are your expenses. You'll bill for your products and services – this is your revenue.

Subtracting your expenses from your revenue yields your net profit. This number is looked at and taxed in differing ways by the IRS depending on your business structure. We'll discuss the details in the following chapter; as a rough estimate for those living in the United States assume that your tax liability will total nearly half your net profit.

That's right; almost half of your net profit will go to taxes. But, there are ways to mitigate this and we'll get into those in the next chapter, don't get too discouraged yet.

Keep meticulous records from the beginning and use a tax professional to help you sort the details to be sure you're abiding by all the rules and taking advantage of everything you possibly can. Hiring professionals to help with this aspect of your business is mandatory. If something goes wrong, you'll need a team of professionals knowledgeable in the details by your side and to ensure this doesn't weigh too far in the negative column.

Availability (-) As a business owner, people have an expectation that you'll always make yourself available and accessible to them.

Some professionals can accept this kind of personal intrusion, some can't. It's important to draw up the boundaries of what you're comfortable with and stick to them. I don't answer my business phone after 4pm and I try to avoid meetings in the evenings or weekends. This balances my availability for my clients and business relationships with my family life.

I've set my business up like this to ensure that I work with people who understand and sympathize with this kind of work-life balance. They're happy to schedule their project meetings around my professional business hours. I look at it this way: I don't demand that my doctor see me when it's most convenient for me, on the weekend. Do you? Why then should someone have that expectation of their architect?

Emotional availability can be tough on your family. Your business can consume much of your mental resources – you're heavily invested in its success. Your family will know when your mind is elsewhere. If you work out of your home and you're one to visit your office frequently, remind yourself of the boundaries you've set for your clients and family, respect your covenants and honor them.

Availability can be a strong negative if you let it.

Design Autonomy (+) If you've worked for someone else for any length of time, you'll greet this as a huge positive. It's your chance to prove your skills. You'll probably find it challenging in different ways. Without input from others, design autonomy can be stress-inducing, especially if you're under pressure to perform for a deadline. Crafting an aesthetic that's uniquely you is not only rewarding but helps distinguish you from your competitors and builds your brand.

Flexibility (+) This was a strong vote in favor of starting my business – a high mass item. Working for yourself means you no longer have to ask for time off, or worry about going for a hike in the middle of the day. You can attend your child's afternoon concert if you choose or grocery shop on a Tuesday morning when no one is there.

Taken in large measure, flexibility, especially without discipline can lead to poor business outcomes. Use it to your advantage not to avoid the work in front of you. I keep a rough schedule outline for each day so the most important business tasks get first crack at my creative stores of energy and are completed first. These are tasks that I develop saying, "If I complete these four things today I will have moved the business forward and it will have been a success."

With limited exception, I 'make' in the mornings and 'manage' in the afternoons. Within that framework, there's flexibility baked in. My children's routine happens in the morning, I exercise in the middle of the day, then more children's activities and homework in the afternoons. I'm present in their lives more than ever because my business allows and prioritizes it.

Financial (+/-) There's great risk and great rewards to be had in owning your own business. It's crucial to structure your business to protect your personal assets as much as possible (hint: it's not a sole-proprietorship). Building is expensive and mistakes are costly. Here's where being pro comes in again. Professional billing rates for professional services demand that you back them up with insurance to safeguard against legal action. A former employer of mine would always say, "Being sued is not a matter of if; it's a matter of when." And even though he operated a small firm of 6, he was involved in a lawsuit for something that he had no purview over. It happens.

The upside is that when you fill your boards with work, or even partially fill them, and set a reasonable billing rate, you'll have given yourself a large pay increase from your previous job. If you practice the lean start-up model, which we'll be discussing, you'll be consistently building a longer and longer runway keeping you in business and profitable.

I'll never forget the first time that I received a $30,000 check in the mail. It took a lot of willpower to keep from running out and buying a new car. Instead, I banked it, deducted the taxes and calculated how much longer that figure would keep my business operating. When played right, these sums can stretch a long way.

Management (-) You probably didn't enter the design field because you excelled at managing. I'm talking about the day-to-day business operations, professional relationships, and employees – none of these responsibilities are easy. Most designers resent the fact that these tasks rob them of design time. But they're essential and they can be turned into a positive if you treat them as their own design project. Develop a conceptual framework, rally the disparate parties, propose solutions, organize, and develop a budget and schedule. Not so bad, right?

Isolation (-) If you'll be practicing on your own, especially if it's out of your home professional isolation is a real mental hurdle you'll need to come to terms with. Even if you consider yourself an introvert, it won't be easy. When I first moved to Maine, where I live and practice now, I transitioned from a very large firm (150+) to working for a firm of eight and it was difficult. In the large firm I had a huge circle of colleagues and entire departments I could learn from and leverage as needed. They had entire divisions dedicated to specification writing, code compliance, presentation, production, and design.

In the smaller firm I had fewer colleagues and far fewer resources to draw upon. Given that the smaller firm was doing solely residential work not all of those resources were necessary, but the personal interactions were welcome especially when I was stuck on a problem and needed an impromptu crit.

If you're a firm of one you'll be responsible for getting all of the work done. You navigate the design challenges and provide the ideas, the innovations, and the brute force. There are ways to mitigate this sense of isolation by using a coworking space, scheduling regular networking events, or meeting other small business owners and like-minded entrepreneurs. Join online communities like: Entrepreneur Architect, The Business of Architecture, Big Time Small Firm, and Archispeak. You can build a circle of friends on platforms like Twitter and Facebook and there's always Skype to solicit feedback from former colleagues or close friends.

Planning your days to force human interaction is another way of not feeling as if you're a hermit. If you have enough work but aren't ready to hire a full-time employee, you can hire from an online community work pool which will ease some of the burden of responsibility for getting everything done that you're bound to resent with time.

In summary, the Pros are:

> Owning your time, flexibility (schedule), financial benefits (set your own rates), no (or limited) commute (owning your time), design autonomy, you build *your* brand (not someone else's), being a business owner, responsibility, and tax advantages.

And the Cons are:

> You're responsible for everything (if it fails it's all on you), business is always there (physically in your home, mentally occupying your thoughts), availability for clients (weekends, evenings, holidays), accounting, invoicing (chasing payments), managing (clients, contractors, you), difficult

phone calls, marketing, financial risk and uncertainty (hardship), fewer vacations, isolation, and tax disadvantages.

This list isn't meant to be all-inclusive; you'll probably have additional factors to consider. But the basics are there. You'll notice that the list of negatives is longer than the list of positives. So the logical question is why would I, or anyone, still choose to make a go of it? For me, it's because the relative mass of the items on the pro list far outweigh the negatives. Time alone is worth more than the sum total of the counterarguments on the con list.

Action Items: I use lists frequently and I encourage you to employ them whenever possible, even if you're the type of person who doesn't rely on lists to accomplish things. The real value in making a list is the mental act of planning that accompanies it.

Develop your own list of the pros and cons of opening your own practice. When you're done, evaluate it and decide whether the positives outweigh the negatives.

Next, define precisely what success would look like to you and write it down. If it's too abstract an exercise, try envisioning what a typical day would look like five years in the future. Or try writing the 'About' page for your future firm's website.

Keep this success statement somewhere visible to you in your workspace as a visible prompt for what's important. In moments of weakness and doubt use it as a reminder of why you're doing what you're doing.

2 | Getting Started

"I move things around until they look right."
– Milton Glaser

Deciding how to structure your business is an early critical decision. I'll begin with a disclaimer - I'm not a lawyer and my advice shouldn't be construed in any way as representing a fully informed legal opinion especially as it relates to your personal circumstances. Hire a lawyer to help you make these decisions for your situation, it's worth it.

Because your choice of business structure will have crucial personal and financial implications, your due diligence is mandatory. At its heart, your business structure defines two basic things: how personal and business assets are treated (owned by you or your business) and your tax strategy. Many people wrongly assume that it protects against liability. If you're a licensed professional (interior designer, structural engineer, architect) you're liable for your professional conduct whether or not you're behind the veil of a corporation.

If you're not a licensed professional there are more protections to be had with differing structures which we'll get into in the following pages.

Start with a basic understanding of the trajectory of your firm. Do you envision becoming the next HOK Sport, with thousands of employees and worldwide offices? Is it just you and a partner? It can be hard to predict where your business will be in one year, let alone five to 10 years, but imagining what success actually looks like may suggest one organizational structure over another.

You may find restrictions geographically that prohibit structuring your business as a corporation, LLC (Limited Liability Corporation) or LLP (Limited Liability Partnership). Transparent ownership and operation of a professional architecture business is generally the goal of these types of restrictions. Check with your state licensing board to research the applicable restrictions for design practices in your location.

As you're researching business structures, here and elsewhere, you'll note the focus on liability. The business structure has some role to play in the assumption of liability, but as I mentioned earlier, as a design professional you are personally liable for your professional acts regardless of how you choose to structure your business. Some financial liability can be assigned to insurers if you choose, but you can never fully assign the liability to anyone else other than you. This is a professional responsibility you must always bear (and be compensated appropriately for).

One final word about the organizing structure as it relates to practicing across state lines. As your business grows to become more globally conscious and connected, you may find yourself practicing in more than one state. Just because your business structure is legal in New York doesn't make it so in California. You must comply with the laws of every state you practice in even if you don't have an office there.

If you're unsure of which structure is right, choose the simplest one to get started; you can grow into the other structures as your business expands.

Sole Proprietorship

Many professionals select sole proprietorship as their initial business structure, because it's simple. It's meant for a single individual without employees. In most cases you won't be required to file any legal creation paperwork with your state, and your Social Security number will used as your tax ID number.

There's a singular disadvantage to a sole proprietorship and it's a big one. Your personal assets and your business assets (and liabilities) are legally viewed as inseparable. This means your home, your car; anything you own can be used as collateral in the event of a lawsuit or legal action. Your personal professional liability is without limit.

Even though there's no legal separation between your personal and professional assets, it's advisable to treat them separately. Although this isn't required by law, it's good business practice. Opening a separate business checking account to handle all business transactions will simplify tax filings and allow the health of your business to be clearly visible and easily monitored. As you grow and decide to move to a different business structure in the future, this separation will make the transition much easier.

Check with your local municipality for specific requirements to be sure you're following all of their rules. The town where I practice required me to file a "Doing Business As" (DBA) form, to prove I was a licensed architect and to pay a small fee. This, in part, is done to ensure they receive any tax revenue that my business may generate.

Starting a sole proprietorship is an easy and immediate process. You can do it today if you'd like. It's a first decision, important yes, but not a final one. You can decide at any point in the future to use a different structure as your business evolves.

Partnership

Businesses are built on the talents of individuals. It's rare that any single person has all the traits necessary to run a successful business; you're likely to be better at some things and worse at others. A partnership leverages these known strengths and weaknesses and shares the responsibility and stress of getting up and running.

If you're not going at this alone, then you are, by default, a legally defined entity called a *partnership*. Drafting a partnership agreement, while not required, is recommended. This is a document that explicitly defines the details of how you'll be operating your firm. Without one, your state will assume each owner is an equal-share partner, and your state's laws based on the Uniform Partnership Act will apply to the business. Portions of the Uniform Partnership Act will apply to your business no matter what, so consulting an attorney is advisable here as well.

At first, when things are going well and everyone is excited about the new venture, the agreement may seem an unnecessary legal expense. But as the business inevitably encounters uncertain times, changing personal situations, or a poor economy, the agreement will protect everyone involved with a predetermined set of rational principles of your own making.

A partnership agreement will include detailed descriptions of things like: ownership stakes (%), initial investment, how to handle profits and losses, decision making, adding or losing owners, liquidation, and dispute resolution, among other things.

The tax implications with this business structure are similar to a sole proprietorship; the net profits of the firm are 'passed through' to each individual according to their ownership stake. Each owner is responsible for paying the tax on their individual tax return.

All of the liability in a partnership extends to each partner. That's 100-percent to each person in the partnership, exactly as if you were a sole proprietor. If you have a partner practicing in another state doing something unscrupulously, you're 100-percent liable for their actions. This is in part the reason for the development of the Limited Liability Partnership (LLP) which we'll discuss later.

Corporations

Here's where things get exponentially more complex. Beneath the corporate banner there are substructures (C-Corp, S-Corp, Professional Corp, etc.) each with a corresponding set of advantages and disadvantages. Again, this is meant to be an overview and shouldn't be construed as legal advice.

With the corporate structure, the personal assets of individual shareholders are separate from the corporation's assets and its creditors. It's a legally separate entity and generally much more complex in its creation, tax filings and maintenance than any other structures. You'll need expert help if you choose this route.

Because the corporation is a separate legal entity, an individual shareholder's personal assets can't be used to fulfill any obligation of the corporation. There are exceptions though: if you personally and directly injure someone, personally guarantee a bank loan, if you don't submit taxes collected from employees to the government, do something intentionally illegal or fraudulent, or treat the corporation as an extension of your personal affairs and not a separate entity.

The last one is important. Failing to do the things that corporations regularly do (directors meetings, issue stock, investing in the corporation, recording business transactions, etc.) is a signal to the IRS that the corporation may be acting as shield from personal liability for its owners (shareholders) and thus not open to the legal protections offered by the corporate structure. In short, do everything that's required of a corporation and you should have no problems. Remember, if you're heavily invested in the corporation those assets are still at risk.

The owners of a corporation are called shareholders. The shareholders elect a board of directors to manage the operations of the corporation and there's a set of bylaws that govern how it operates. Unlike a publicly traded corporation whose shares are sold and traded on the open market, a private corporation's shares are bought and sold privately.

Usually, but not always, the shareholders of private corporations are also employees of the company and oversee the daily operations of the business. For this work they receive a salary like other employees, that's commensurate with their level of experience and contributions. As a shareholder, they will also receive distributions of the profits (or losses) of the corporation.

From a tax standpoint the corporation is a separate entity and must file its own tax return and the individual shareholders must also file their own tax returns. Because both the individual shareholders and the corporation must pay tax on the profits (income tax), the profits of a corporation are at risk of double taxation. Paying bonuses out to employees and shareholders to distribute the profits at year-end is one way around this double taxation. By doing this the corporation zeroes out their profits leaving nothing to tax.

Another way around double taxation is to leverage subsection 'S' in the IRS tax code. This is the genesis of the 'S-Corp' - a structure that passes the profits of the corporation through to the individual owners leaving the corporation itself with little (or no) tax obligation. This affords the shareholders the financial protections of the corporation with the simplicity of the sole proprietor's tax reporting.

As you might imagine, the filings for establishing and maintaining a corporation are far greater than any other structure. Choosing this structure may actually affect the name of your firm too. Architecture firms in California must contain the name of one of the founders or owners and the word Architect or Architects. There are annual reports to write and shareholders' meetings to conduct and you're required to issue stock. Although it's more complex, the legal and tax advantages often outweigh the extra work involved. When a business scales beyond a few individuals and employees it's a logical -- almost mandatory -- progression for a growing design practice.

LLC/LLP

Limited liability corporations (LLCs) and limited liability partnerships (LLPs) offer the protections of a corporation (limited liability) combined with the simplicity of pass-through taxation of sole proprietorship or the S-Corp. Your liability as an owner is limited to the amount you've invested in the company – if it fails that's the amount you'll lose.

Single-member LLCs are a subset that the IRS treats slightly differently. By default, the IRS will classify and tax your business as if you're a sole proprietor. This means you'll pay self-employment tax on all your net earnings. You can, however, elect to be taxed as a corporation if you choose.

Multi member LLCs are treated as partnerships, again, unless the partners elect to be treated as a corporation. The partners are each taxed as individuals on their income-tax returns.

NOTE: If you elect to be taxed as a corporation when you form your LLC/LLP you won't be able to change it for a period of 60 months. Choose wisely.

The possible advantage of electing to be taxed as a corporation (specifically the S-Corp) is that the owner(s) then receives a salary with the LLC paying the payroll tax and any excess profit (distributed via dividends) isn't subjected to self-employment tax. The C-Corp structure allows the LLC to retain all the earnings within the business and not pass on any of the profits, which can help defer tax liability when facing potentially higher tax brackets.

Just because it's possible to realize some tax savings doesn't make it a good strategy. The extra accounting and tax filing costs involved and increased scrutiny of the IRS all makes this difficult to recommend to a young business. You have enough to worry about securing and doing the work without the added burden of complicated tax structures.

Neither of these organizations is a separate tax entity – like a corporation. The LLC/LLP doesn't file a tax return; rather the individual does, claiming the profits and losses from the LLC/LLP on his or her personal tax return.

The liability protections are similar to the corporation in that the owner(s) of the LLC/LLP can't be held personally liable for any lawsuits, judgments or debt related to the business.

Many sole proprietors transition to the LLC as their workload and exposure to risk increases. The expanded protection is traded for additional paperwork. For a small fee, sites like LegalZoom can help you complete and submit the necessary forms.

Operating Agreement. It's advisable to file an operating agreement though most states don't require it (only five do). The agreement sets out the terms and rules for operating your business and helps protect your limited liability status. The operating agreement for the LLC/LLP offers you the chance to expressly state the ownership stakes and distribution of profits and losses.

For example, if you and a partner enter into an agreement whereby you contribute 20% of the working capital and 80% of the work, and your partner contributes 80% of the working capital and 20% of the work you can elect to share the profits 50/50. In a corporation that flexibility wouldn't be allowed, each would be compensated based on their actual contribution percentages.

A reminder. Please seek legal counsel to determine the best fit for your business and personal situation. I'm not a business lawyer and neither are you. Paying for professional advice is worth every penny. Lawyers can tell you whether the structure you're considering is allowed. For example, in some states, such as California, the LLC and LLP structure isn't allowed for licensed architects, there you'll have to incorporate or act as a sole proprietor.

Tax Basics

Selecting a business structure is as much about choosing how to organize the business, as it is a decision about how that business, and by extension you, will be taxed. This is one area that the IRS is very clear about: a Corporation, by definition, is a distinct entity and one that's taxed separately from its owners. The sole proprietorship, S-Corp, and LLC/LLP organizations are set up so that the profits and losses are 'passed through' to the business owner to claim on their individual tax forms.

Always remember that revenue minus expenses equals profit. For accounting purposes, when you transfer money from your business account this should be recorded in your accounting software as an 'Owner Drawing'. In your former life as an employee this was like payday. The difference is, now you can do this whenever you'd like.

Maintaining separate accounts allows you to track the information and aid you in creating your profit and loss sheet when it's time to pay taxes. If this sounds extremely complicated, it's not. A good accounting program will generate your profit and loss sheet for you assuming you've been good about tracking it along the way.

Estimated Taxes. In the United State the tax system is a pay-as-you-go arrangement. As an employee, you probably noticed that your net earnings every two weeks were smaller than your gross earnings. This difference was your incremental tax payment. As a business owner, you must pay taxes on your profit each quarter. Tax deadlines are: January 15, April 15, June 15, and September 15 and your payment is due to the Federal government and your State on these dates. You can choose to set these up to electronically debit on the exact date or send a check by mail – I prefer online payment for its electronic paper trail.

For a new business, estimated taxes can be difficult to figure out because you'll have no history to reference. The IRS has an estimated tax calculator on their website which is hard to understand and poorly designed. The advice I received from my accountant for year one was to set aside roughly half of my profit for taxes each quarter. At the end of the tax year this netted me a healthy refund and at that point I had the information I needed to file the following year's estimated taxes.

Deductions. See the IRS website for a complete list.

1. Car/Truck Expenses. You can elect to deduct either the actual mileage used for business or keep a detailed accounting of the expenses related to the maintenance and upkeep of a vehicle used for

business. If the vehicle is used for anything other than business, you'll need to allocate the associated costs on a percentage basis. Tracking mileage is the simplest; make sure it's a log that's contemporaneous and kept either in the vehicle or on your phone. I use Evernote for this.
2. Depreciation. When you invest in equipment or assets that have a useful life greater than one year you must depreciate the value of these items and deduct their expense over their useful life. Section 179 of the tax code allows you to depreciate the full value of the expense in the year it was incurred up to a specific dollar amount.
3. Travel, meals, entertainment. Keep meticulous records including the names of people in attendance and the project it was related to. Read up on the many rules you must abide by to make sure your expenses qualify.
4. Business use of home (home office deduction). You must have a part of your home that you use regularly and exclusively for your business. Measure its dimensions and to calculate its size as a percentage of your overall home. Then you'll need to tally all the expenses for your home and multiply it by this percentage.
5. Subscriptions.
6. Advertising.
7. Business-related gifts.

NOTE: Taxes are not a business expense.

Self-employment Tax. Here's another tax you probably weren't aware of as an employee. Sole proprietors must also pay into the Social Security and Medicare systems in the United States. These taxes combined are known as the self-employment tax and they equal the FICA (Federal Insurance Contributions Act) tax an employee and corporation pays on an employee's earnings. When you were an employee half this amount was paid by you and your employer paid the other half. As a sole proprietor, you're required to pay the entire amount. In 2014 the self-employment tax was 15.3% on the first $117,000 of income and 2.9% on everything exceeding that amount

When your yearly tax filing comes around you'll be able to deduct half the self-employment tax from your personal income.

Tax and the Individual. The pass-through structures described above (Sole Proprietor, Partnership, & LLC/LLP) all require the individual to report their share of the business profits and losses on their personal income-tax return using a *Schedule C*. This is the IRS form used to quantify your business' income and your expenses. The Schedule C is an itemized list of your income and expenses. Simply stated, your business' income minus expenses equals profit (or loss). This is the amount that will be added to your personal taxable income.

As a sole proprietor, I found the concept of 'taking a paycheck' or drawing money out of the business, at least initially, to be confusing. The business would generate income that I would deposit into the business bank account. I reasoned that I could leave that money there indefinitely and draw on it as I needed it. That much was true. However, I also thought that if I personally didn't transfer the money from the business account to my personal account then I didn't have to consider it profit (thus owing taxes on that profit). My accountant dispelled this myth immediately as inaccurate. Income minus expenses equals profit or loss. The IRS calculates the tax due based on two things: when you earn the money during the year and your net profit. The IRS doesn't care where you *keep* your earnings; you can transfer them to your personal account, or stash them under your mattress. They only care *when* you earned it and how much you earned.

The way the IRS looks at your business profits is in one of two ways and it's based on the accounting method you select on your Schedule C. You didn't take an accounting class you say? Me either. It's quite simple though. Each time you file your Schedule C, you'll need to choose either the *accrual method* or the *cash method* of accounting. With the accrual method, you account for income as you earn it. With the cash method of accounting, you account for the income when you actually receive it. That is, when you physically have it in your possession. Once you select the accrual method of accounting for your business you must stick with it, however, with the cash method you can change to accrual whenever you'd like – but, there's no going back.

Although these methods sound similar, there's an important distinction. You may earn the money well before you're compensated. As an example, let's say you complete a set of drawings in November and invoice your client during my next billing cycle at the end of the month. Your client may not get around to paying you until after the first of the following year. Remember, with the accrual method of accounting, you must pay the tax due on the income as you earn it. This means that when you pay your fourth-quarter estimated taxes you must pay the tax due on the accrued income – even if it's before you've been paid.

With the cash method, you don't have to pay the tax on the income until you have payment in hand. If you receive it before the end of the year, you'll include it on that year's tax filings. If you don't, you're not forced to come up the funds to pay the taxes out of your own pocket until your client decides to pay the bill. It's a big advantage for a new business getting on its feet.

For my business, I find cash accounting the most straightforward. It allows more control over the timing of tax liabilities as well. I can choose the most convenient time to invoice for work completed and collect the debts owed to me. Without too much effort you can imagine possibilities where this may work to your advantage, particularly as the tax year (or quarter) comes to a close.

As a new business owner finances will be tight, you'll probably appreciate the flexibility that the cash method provides too. Speak with your tax preparer and accountant for a professional opinion, as your own situation is likely to be more nuanced.

One other thing to note when selecting an accounting method is that the accrual method is the one that allows you to write off bad debt on your taxes. When you invoice for work completed and a client doesn't pay, it's considered *uncollectible* or *bad debt*. Bad debt can be treated as a business expense but only if you use the accrual method of accounting. With cash accounting, you can't claim it as bad debt because you haven't paid the tax on it; the IRS never knew you earned it.

You'll undoubtedly have some bad debt, but it should be small compared to your other earnings and it shouldn't be enough to outweigh the benefits of the cash accounting method.

Tax and the Corporation. By contrast, the IRS considers corporations to be separate entities from its owners. This means that an individual isn't taxed on the corporation's earnings. Similar to the individual, the corporation must pay tax on its net profits. The amount of money left over after all salaries, bonuses, overhead and expenses are paid determines how much the corporation is taxed. It's important to note that the corporate tax rate differs from the individual tax rate.

Profits left in the business and not distributed to owners (or employees) are called retained earnings. These are subjected to the corporate tax rate, but don't flow to the shareholders as dividends, bonuses or salaries. These funds can be used to capitalize the corporation, to fund growth, or for another tax strategy.

Like the individual, the corporation has legitimate expenses it can deduct including start-up costs, operating expenses, advertising, equipment, salaries, bonuses and benefits paid out to employees. Because the salary and bonus expenses are deductible and not subject to taxation, the issue of double taxation is nullified.

Your clients will be paying the corporation and not you the individual. You, the individual, will pay tax on the distributions the corporation makes to you in the form of a salary, bonus or dividend. This is complex, but important to understand as your business grows.

Here's where it can really pay to involve a tax professional as an advisor. I'm not a tax professional, only a taxpayer; so take this advice for what it is. The corporation does have some special tax advantages. As a shareholder in a corporation, you can be an owner and an employee. Employees can receive salaries and bonuses. Shareholders can also receive dividends. Now, remember the self-employment tax? That tax applies to *earned income* – money paid to you as an employee – your salary and bonuses.

Corporations can structure compensation packages to take advantage of the tax rules regarding dividends by opting for a reduced (but 'reasonable') salary – let's say 60% which is supplemented with a dividend package for the remaining 40%. This can be an effective and perfectly legal way to limit the amount of self-employment tax paid on a portion of one's income.

In this example, the corporation still must pay the half of the employment tax due (which is deductible for the corporation) and the individual must pay half of the employment tax due on the salary. The C-Corp (regular corporation) must also account for the dividends as regular income and pay corporate tax on the dividends it distributes. For this strategy to be most effective, it must be used with the S-Corp structure. With the S-Corp, the dividends *do* offset corporate income and this tax can be avoided.

As an example, if you assume a $90,000 base salary and divide it into $50,000 in salary and $40,000 in dividends you'll save $6,120 per year in taxes. This is because you're not subjecting $40,000 of your income to the 15.3% self-employment tax. You'll also be able to deduct half of your self-employment tax as an expense, which means that half of the 15.3% of the $50,000 salary – $3,825 ($7650 / 2) – can be deducted from the $50,000 leaving $46,175 as taxable income instead of the $50,000. The self-employment tax is the same, but the total tax liability is lower.

Other implications of these approaches can be hard to quantify; things like the amount of Social Security benefits you'll be allowed to collect in the future, how losses and debts are handled, and your potential chances of being audited. Whenever the IRS stands to lose tax revenue you can be assured they're keeping a careful eye on the structures that permit easy abuse. Saving a few thousand dollars can seem attractive when margins are tight but the trade-off in fines, penalties and a professional defense can quickly erase any financial savings replacing them with mental anguish and a bankrupted business.

If this all sounds complicated it's because it is. Please seek the help of a professional to determine the implications for your situation. You don't want to be caught on the wrong side of an IRS audit.

Action Items: Select a business structure and file the necessary paperwork.

What works for me: When I first started, like many professionals, I chose sole proprietorship. However, now that my business is a few years old and my exposure to risk and my profits are substantially greater than they were in the past, I'm considering moving to the LLC structure taxed as a corporation. The LLC will be less expensive to initiate, provide me with increased personal asset protections, limit the paperwork associated my business operations, and the S-Corp structure will allow me additional tax-planning flexibility.

Licensing & Regulations

The next procedural step along the way is to determine what you'll need to legally practice in your state and local municipality. Because interior design and architecture are regulated professions, your state will have laws and rules and a board of licensure. Your state licensing board is a good first point of contact to learn exactly what's required of professionals acting in your capacity in your state. Before you can actually do the work, you'll need to secure any permits or licenses required to practice.

Having a professional license isn't a requirement to practice single-family residential architecture in most states. However, if you're not licensed, you need to know the rules that govern your area before getting started. If you're taking your exams but aren't licensed yet, you might consider partnering with another firm in your area as a way of building credibility and experience in a particular niche market.

If you're not a licensed professional, it's important that you don't present yourself as one. Don't call yourself an 'Architect' or 'Interior Designer' if you're not licensed. This means anywhere and in any form: orally, written, online, business card, e-mail signature or on your letterhead. Not only are you misrepresenting yourself to the public; but you could face censure, fines, and penalties and possibly prevent your future self from ever becoming licensed.

Licensing is a legal process designed to protect the health and safety of the general public; it's a serious business. As harmless as it may seem, calling yourself an Architect without the legal backing is asking for trouble.

Annual license renewal fees and the cost of NCARB (National Council of Architectural Registration Board) record keeping can total in the hundreds of dollars per year, depending on where you live. Make sure to track these as business expenses. When it's time to pay your taxes each quarter you'll account for them in your financial statement.

Business model
This is simply your plan to earn revenue. Historically, design practices have been solely based on the consulting model. Although the means of compensation differ under this structure - hourly, fixed fee, percentage of cost - at its core, consulting links time (billable hours) directly to revenue. It's still a very popular choice among new business owners because it works and clients expect it.

But, there are some real disadvantages to pursuing the consulting model. Chief among them is that trading time for dollars is the least effective way to scale a business. This is because time is a finite resource; you have a fixed amount of time in a week you can invoice for. To scale your revenues, you must do one of two things: increase billing rates or hire (lower wage/higher margin) employees. With the hourly consulting model, you'll reach a point where you can't increase your hourly billing rate without pricing your service out of the market. Worse yet, this model will keep you working for the business rather than on the business. If you don't show up to do the work, the revenue stops.

Entrepreneurial thinking can transform the way you choose to design your practice. The constraint of the consulting business model is arbitrary. Look to other businesses in the world for inspiration and ways around tying your time to income. To unhitch your business from the hourly consulting model requires thinking about the deliverables of your service through a different lens. We've grown so accustomed to providing one-off, bespoke consulting services, tailored to an individual – typically wealthy – client's needs, that we've neglected to see what the rest of the market has already noticed.

People buy *products*.

Why? Because there's an immediate value judgment we can make when we look at a product, it's a binary decision. Yes the value is clear or no it isn't. I'll gladly pay $1,200 for a Gary Fisher mountain bike because I know what I'm getting. I can take it for a test ride, it feels comfortable, I like the geometry. It's a physical product with tangible, known qualities.

Contrast this with an unfamiliar service – hiring an interior designer or architect. How can we expect a client to place a value on that service? We can't. The client inherently looks at your service as a cost rather than value because they typically have no frame of reference. Design as a service is intangible and coupled with its high cost it's no wonder the value proposition is unclear to the average consumer. That's the trouble with a consulting business model and it's one you'll bump up against continually if you choose this route.

Knowing this, what are some alternative business models? How about products? Or productized services (a fixed-fee service with defined deliverables) with monthly recurring revenue streams? Think about the design products we can create once and sell in the market repeatedly. Businesses create products for sale all the time. The bakery offers doughnuts for sale each morning and the selling price reflects a sensible (baked-in) overhead and profit. With this model we have to make the value proposition clear, but assuming we're able to move product, the business is guaranteed to survive because the price is set in a way that rewards our efficiencies.

Unfortunately, I don't have a solution or an answer as to what will work for you, or even whether this is the right model for your business. What you should sell or how much to sell it for is a decision that you'll have to make. There is no one-size-fits-all solution for our profession. Yet the business model for the practicing design professional has resisted change for too long; it hasn't evolved with our consumer economy. If your business can connect with a consumer, you'll thrive. Your new business can capitalize on this opportunity.

Now, it's your turn to apply your creativity to the challenge. Here are a few thoughts to prime your inner idea machine and set you off creatively developing novel ways for a design practice to produce revenue.

- Deliver BIM models as a product: leverage your knowledge of BIM to manage an outsourced team to create existing conditions models for institutional clients.

- Productized service for monthly fee. Unlimited design consults for a fixed, recurring monthly fee (interiors, architecture, color selection, furniture). Think about realty services you offer for a fixed fee. Business-to-Business marketing is ideal, they're not afraid to spend money to make money.

- Develop (design/build) your own work and sell it.

- Branded renovations / property flips.

- White-label a product line. Select among products being manufactured in China via Alibaba (hardware, lights, and accessories), brand them with your label and sell them online directly through fulfillment by Amazon (FBA).

- Create a new product line. Hardware, fabrics, lighting.

- Design an app around the building products industry. Make someone's life easier (another business preferably). Think about those with more money than time: contractors, building owners, realtors, and facilities managers.

- Design residential plan sets with embedded affiliate links to key interior products (see Chapter 5 on Internet marketing).

- Write books for sale on digital marketplaces (architecture, plan books, design tips, color theory)

- Sell specification books for high performance home design.

- Manage an outsourced team of CAD professionals.

- Curate an online store of "Architect's Favorite" products with revenue from ads and affiliate commission links.

- Specialize: become the prefab or container house guru, the 'Sonos for your home' resource. Build a product line around this specialty.

- Lead architecture-based trips around the world.

- Teach design courses. Udemy or Lynda. Course could be software specific or design centric, find a niche and build a course around it.

Imagine how it would feel to be earning while you sleep, while you play with your children, while you're on vacation. A passive income model is limitless in scale. By developing products or productized services to generate revenue while you do other things, you can build this opportunity into your business from the start.

If you're not ready to take any of the above on in the beginning, you should at least recognize the limitations of a business that marries your time to income. Pivoting is a theme we'll return to often in this book, it's a necessary business skill. Start with a service-based consulting model (hourly billing) and work toward building passive income streams along the way. You'll then have the opportunity to pivot when the stream becomes a river.

Insurance

Depending on the exact type of work you're seeking, where you'll be practicing, your business structure and specific client needs, you may be required to purchase insurance. There are many types of insurance you may want to consider when you open your practice: health insurance, life insurance, property insurance, and the king of them all: professional liability insurance.

Ask any professional who has been in business long enough and they're bound to have at least one story about a relationship that ended in an unforeseen financial obligation. Nobody plans to make mistakes or have an accident, but they happen all the time. Without professional liability insurance, your business must secure the debt of the loss. If you're a sole proprietor, this can be particularly devastating as your personal assets are all at risk – your home, your car, your drafting table, and your computers. Everything.

Here's where your business structure can protect you to a degree. The LLC/LLP and Incorporated businesses must secure the loss but that doesn't pass along to the owners or shareholders.

Insurance is always a good idea if you can afford it — to cover not only errs and omissions but also liability. Some say you can't afford *not* to have insurance. Just starting out it may be difficult to quantify just how much insurance you need and what type of deductible you can afford.

Professional liability insurance is very expensive - until you need it. A design professional assumes many risks, many of which are beyond our control. When something goes wrong on a job-site or even at the office (think employees or clients visiting) there's always finger pointing. The Contractor blames the Architect, the Architect blames the Contractor, and the Owner blames both.

Even if a problem stems from a clearly defined, single responsible party often others will be drawn into a legal proceeding. If you're working on large contracts with large sums of money at stake, you can be assured that the other parties will have insurance companies (most are required to by law) and their lawyers looking for a financial settlement.

Having insurance doesn't relieve you of all financial obligations when a claim arises. Your deductible, any amounts in excess of your coverage, and things your policy doesn't cover remain your responsibility.

To purchase insurance you'll want to contact a broker specializing in design related fields. They can help you ask the right questions and shop around for a policy that balances affordability and appropriateness. Your premium will be based on: your exposure to liability, the number of employees you have, your (and any employees) experience level, your deductible, the type of work you do, your annual billings, and various other unknowable factors.

To give you an idea of cost, a small firm can expect to pay roughly $5,000 annually for $1M in coverage with a $5,000 deductible. This would mean paying the first $5,000 out of pocket for any claim. Although policies differ, basic coverage provides legal representation at no additional cost (subject to the deductible and policy limits). A lawyer's typical hourly rate is between $400-500 per hour – imagine paying for that out of pocket.

Lower deductibles are available, but there's a trade-off between cost and coverage. The deductible is on a per claim basis, not an annual deductible you may be accustomed to with your health-insurance policy.

When you seek coverage from an insurance company at any point you'll need to discuss how current liabilities are covered. Insurance companies call these, Prior Acts. You can purchase separate coverage for these but coverage is generally not retroactive. This almost always comes up as firms seek coverage after a problem has been made known. You're unlikely to receive any coverage for that circumstance. Make sure you're clear on the terms of your coverage before agreeing to it including termination and how coverage is handled if you move on from this business to another.

The AIA maintains an excellent resource called AIA Trust on all things insurance and financial. It's designed specifically for architects and I've found it quite helpful. If you're an AIA member ($600-700/year) you can also subscribe to LegaLine, a legal advice hotline available exclusively to AIA members. It's a subscription based service with very affordable rates: $175 for 3 months, $300 for 6 months, 1 year for $500.

Your insurance expenses will be weighed against your cash flow when you head out on your own. Following a lean start-up model requires that you assume risk, especially in the start-up stage.

Action Items: Choose a business model. Consider at least one idea for generating passive income to work on over time. Research your local business licensing, filing and insurance requirements and fees. Account for these in an initial start-up budget.

What works for me: I chose the consulting model as a first step because I already had clients I was working with. Over time, I've been developing my passive income streams through a process of trial and error. Currently, I sell a line of plan sets on my website, publish videos on YouTube (monetized with Adsense), post content online with embedded affiliate links, I offer productized service packages, and I write digital content for purchase (this book is one example).

I'm always trying new things and looking for ways to maintain my runway and keep the business profitable. No single passive business model would keep the business fully funded and operational, but together they reach a critical mass that leaves room for more experimentation. I offer this as inspiration to you to take action. You can leverage your skills to produce income for you while you focus on other activities.

On the practical side, I filed a DBA with my local town and verified the requirements for practice with my State Licensing Board. Their only requirements were that I maintain my license (by paying an annual fee) and use the term, "Licensed Maine Architect" on all my correspondence (e-mails, letters, and official documents). I'm not required to carry professional liability insurance and I currently have no plans to purchase it. I can sleep at night, but there's a twinge of fear when problems arise on a job-site. I try to mitigate the risk by carefully selecting clients and contractors to partner with.

3 | Your Brand

"A genius is the one most like himself."
-Thelonious Monk

It's time to discuss your business plan. I forgive you for groaning, that was actually my reaction too every time I heard the word business plan mentioned to me by family or friends, "Have you written your business plan yet?" This book won't teach you how to write a business plan.

Instead of developing a business plan no one will ever read, you'll be defining your brand. If you're into writing business plans, by all means, you should. If you're seeking financing or venture backing, you'll probably need one. But it isn't necessary; you don't need to borrow money to start your firm when you follow lean start-up principles.

The business plan seeks to make real an unknowable future. Do I think you should do some basic math to figure out what you need to earn, who your target market is, and how you plan to make a financially informed best effort? Sure, you need a few foundational metrics to begin. But that's about all. In Chapter 8 we'll discuss personal and operational finances in detail.

The false assumption that a twelve-page business plan with supporting figures and revenue projections is required before getting started can be an enormous barrier. Don't let it be the thing that keeps you from moving forward; you're going to learn and pivot along the way. The only way to figure most things a business plan seeks to define is to start doing them. After the first month any draft business plan will be irrelevant anyhow.

Defining your brand is no less challenging than writing a business plan. But it's a task that can be approached as a design project. When I talk about "brand," I'm not talking about what your logo or your letterhead or your business cards look like — although those are parts of it— I really mean, what does your business stand for?

When you think of Apple Computer, you probably have an image formed in your mind of their brand, perhaps it's their logo, a Macbook Pro, or an iPhone. Apple's brand message, the image that precedes their product, is clear: exceptionally well-designed, personal electronics. It's clear because everything Apple does is in support of this message. Their advertising, their form-factor, their website, their stores, their packaging – each is designed to remind you of what they do well.

Although Apple is an excellent example, there are plenty of others to look to for inspiration as you're defining your brand. Sometimes it can be useful to look to smaller businesses, ones that look more like you to remind you that Jobs and Wozniak started Apple Computer in a garage.

Thinking about what your brand will say is your first task; one that precedes even the naming your firm. What would be the tagline of your website or book? What's the narrative? What makes you unusual? What need are you fulfilling? Whose problem are you solving? What's your origin story? These are some questions that can lead to defining a strong brand.

Let's use my practice, 30X40 Design Workshop, as an example. My work draws inspiration from the humble agricultural and industrial structures — barns, sheds, farmhouses — that populate rural America. I've always admired their simple shapes and their narrative qualities and how clearly they describe what was important to their creators so visibly through their architecture. The name 30X40 is drawn from the classic dimensions of the New England threshing barn — 30 feet by 40 feet. The size and interior layout correlated with the proportion of a team of oxen. The center bay allowed the farmer to load the barn with hay by driving his wagon through the large doors and provided a central workspace.

While that's the origin of the brand name, the more important subtext is that the name elicits a question. "Why 30X40?" And the story unfolds from there; a story about place, structure and ideas. It's precisely this process of digging deeper and the telling of stories latent in people and places that's the broader goal of my work as an architect. Appending "Design Workshop" suggested to me a process of informally testing ideas. Workshops are messy places where there's freedom to experiment, to construct, to test, revise and retest. My studio, the place where I greet clients, is then the physical manifestation and metaphorical link to the brand title, a true "Design Workshop."

I developed the story as a starting point; a place to begin building my brand. And, although I started there, with time it's evolved. Simple, modern, idea-driven design was a tagline I used for a while. Now I've changed it to site-specific, craft-driven, residential architecture. I'll probably change it again, and again, and again. The point is, I'm never satisfied with my business, I always want it to be a more accurate reflection of what I'm thinking about and what I'm doing today, but the underlying core remains the same. I tell stories about places and people using walls, columns, floors, roofs and the raw materials of building. I design simple, modern homes that tell a story.

It's not important that you develop an exact story to describe the origin of your firm name as I did. But you need a brand story to tell and ideally it would be something you can deliver in a single sentence. Thinking in taglines is a good place to start. Make it something your spouse, your friends or your parents can easily relay to friends and family. Imagine it to be something a 6-year old would be able to understand. That doesn't mean it should be generic or trite, just clear. Describe benefits not features. What do you do that impacts people's lives? How will your business change the world?

When defining your brand, conceptually speaking, you're acting as the client and the architect. You'll choose the site first (your niche), then you'll decide where to place it on that site (what makes you unique), then you'll decide what it will look like (your brand). Think about what can set your business apart. Why start your own firm at all? What do you bring to the world that no one else does?

One helpful exercise is to list all the things you're interested in on a sheet of paper. Begin drawing connections between each interest, hybridizing them and highlighting what's extraordinary about your way of seeing the world. What's your lens? Travel, wood joinery, brewing, graphics, writing, teaching, architecture, games, hiking, laser cutting, typography, trainspotting, and photography were a few of the interests on my list. Drawing lines between interests nets something about me as an individual and a mine of niches to begin thinking about new business ideas.

What's distinctive about you? If you answer with, "I'm a gifted designer," you're probably not alone and I'm sure you are. But the world is full of talented designers; that can't be your differentiator. People have a limited lexicon when it comes to architecture and interior design; they have no internal framework for judging design talent.

There's no question that people care about design, now probably more than they ever have in history, but really what people want in an architect or designer is someone who will creatively solve their problems. It's not about you. You'll be judged on how well clients think you'll be able to solve their very personal needs, not on how well composed your portfolio looks or your design skills. You need a strong portfolio to open the door, but it's your ability to communicate to clients that you care about their problems and can capably offer solutions to meet their immediate needs that matters.

For many, branding begins by picturing an ideal client. How does your firm specifically cater to the needs of that client? Whose problem does your business solve? Think specifics. Don't fall into the generalist trap. Trying to solve everyone's problems is a shortcut to solving no one's. Begin by solving the very specific needs of one group of people first. Be the ultimate resource for their problems. How can your brand offer a pointed solution to their pressing needs?

Do you have experience in passive house design or historic renovations, multi-family housing, or Brownfield development? Remember to describe benefits and not features. If you're still stuck, try studying the companies you admire with a strong brand and note the characteristics of their brand that you'd most like to emulate.

You might try asking those around you about the qualities they associate with you. Ask them to be specific. Do you see a theme emerging? Try to build on that.

It's important to understand that everything you do contributes toward the building of your brand. Your brand precedes you.

Recognize this even in simple daily tasks — sending an e-mail, how you word your contract or construct the *About* page on your website, and of course posting to social media. Your brand speaks for you when you're not there. It's a powerful partner in delivering your message.

The Name. Your business name will be the first thing that will greet prospective clients, the centerpiece of your brand, and it's a powerful positioning strategy. Don't spend more than a day on the naming exercise, it's important but you'll need to get started on building your marketing strategy around the business name as soon as possible.

Note: depending on where you live, your state's practice act may require you to include the founder's last name along with the word Architect, Architects, or Architecture in the firm name. Don't let this scuttle your plans for a better name, simply register your firm name according to your state's rules, then register your fictitious name or DBA (Doing Business As) to change it to your new (more creative) name of choice.

A few approaches to consider:

> **Last Name(s).** The classic solution to the naming problem is to use your own name. Combining the last names of the founding or current partners persists as one of the most common, and possibly least creative, naming conventions for professional firms.
>
> I've worked for many firms who adopted this approach. I recall one in particular with three last names followed by 'Architecture.' It was a tongue twister and answering the phone became a 20 second affair that usually ended with clients on the other end chuckling. Relaying my e-mail address – more than 30 characters long - was an equally comical exercise.
>
> Although this is a safe approach to naming, it reminds me of a law or accounting firm in its creative resolution. Think too about how your firm may outgrow its founding partner(s). Initially all clients will have the opportunity to work with person whose name is on the sign. Consider how a client may react when they hire Renzo Piano but can't work with him.
>
> Abbreviations are an improvement when there's more than one partner (HOK, SOM) but they risk being cutesy in their wordplay.

ARCHITECT + ENTREPRENEUR

1 - **Studio, Atelier, Collaborative, Collective, Lab, Agency, Bureau, Office.** Adding any of these nouns after your last name is a more contemporary and popular version of the first convention. It does suggest some exclusivity and conceit that may be off-putting to some but attractive to others. Of course, you can add these nouns to another word or phrase just don't confuse people about what service you offer.

2 - **Design, Interior Design, Architecture.** Imagine answering the phone. Design is fine, but it's not a professionally regulated term, anyone can append this to their name. Architecture, however, is a regulated term – you can't use it unless you're a registered professional. It's also quite a mouthful.

3 - **Associates, Architects.** I think the term Architects can actually work well for a partnership, it's simple and direct. But it's hard to pull off if you're a firm of one and somewhat awkward with three. Your client may question whether they'll be working with you or one of your unnamed 'Associates.'

4 - **Random Meaningful (to you) Name.** I chose a name supported by a narrative that had meaning to me. This strategy may work for you and resonate with clients or it may fall flat. You can use this as a differentiator from the competition. My approach was to combine this strategy with approach number one above. I subscribed to the notion that when given a choice between something that has a story associated with it and one that doesn't people will more often choose the one with a story. Recognize though that it's a business name and the story they're looking for is the one you'll be writing about *them* through your design.

5 - **Punctuation: + / & -- | { } [ ] .** You might as well give it a try. I don't actually think this is particularly helpful or harmful. Graphically they're nice elements, but the plus sign can also be read as an "and" so make sure there's no confusion. Imagine answering the phone, is it a 'plus' or an "and"? Finding a domain name can be more complex too, for example, the 'X' in 30X40 Design Workshop. I spelled it out for my Internet domain, but it's more complex than necessary.

6 - **Random Capitalization.** It's a TrAp! You may satisfy an inner need for a clever graphical solution but you risk a

client questioning how to pronounce your name. You're not a typographer, save this one for them.

7 - (Parenthetical Insertions) Don't get too creative; nobody will get it but you. When I see firms named 'Design l(A)b' or 'ARChitectURE' it seems as though they're trying too hard. See also number 4 above – it's your baby; the final decision lies with you.

Naming will either be a simple exercise for you or a really difficult one. There's a comprehensive guide to check out if you need focused help or if you're just genuinely interested in the psychology of naming. You can find it at: www.igorinternational.com/process. The IGOR guide offers six clearly defined steps to developing your own.

Because your business name is your public face, you'll want to think beyond the basics of just answering the office phone. How will you introduce yourself? Hi, I'm Eric, Founder of (Insert business name). Make it something you can easily and repeatedly say. You'll also want to choose a name that lends itself to web development. Do a quick check to verify whether the online domain (.com .net) is available for purchase. If it isn't, consider changing it.

What works for me: Having discussed the origins of my brand earlier, I can confess that if I had this to do over I'd probably choose a different name. I violated a few of the rules we just discussed, but I've also made peace with the decision. The three biggest mistakes I made were:

A) **Meaning.** Having to explain what 30X40 means to new a client is cumbersome and not everyone understands it even after I'm done explaining. A good name does the explaining for you.

B) **Length.** The name is too long. I've adopted the shortened version, 30X40, when introducing myself or answering the phone.

C) **Not Search Engine Optimized (SEO).** With some experience now developing web properties I realize what a rookie mistake this was. My business domain is: thirtybyforty.com, which correlates with "30X40 Design Workshop." The first problem is verbally relaying to people the URL - I have to spell it out or most assume its 30x40. The second, and bigger problem, is that I receive search traffic from people intending to build a 30' by 40' workshop – quite a bit of search traffic in fact. To Google, I look like an architect who designs 30-foot by 40-foot workshops. The traffic comes because I rank highly for the term, but they quickly leave after realizing that it's not what I do. This is bad for SEO (search engine optimization) and means I'm less likely to reach my target audience. SEO is a critical element to your marketing strategy (see Chapter 5 for a detailed description) even if you're going to focus on a local market and you feel it's not as important. For the business I'm building, I need the SEO to market my business globally.

Look at your competition's websites, at their branding. What does it say about their business? How can you say it better? How can you distinguish yourself from them? What do you do that they can't? Perhaps you're the anti-brand.

A brand takes time to establish and you actually don't get the final say. A brand is what people perceive it to be. Remember that even big brands, the Apples and Coca-Colas of the world, started right where you are today. Brands evolve and yours will too; you have to start small by thinking about what you want your brand to say.

Action Items: Begin defining your brand. Think about your company name. Develop an ideal client avatar and a tagline; in the next chapter we'll begin crafting your brand's online presence to accurately tell your story. For now, it's enough to know a few things:

1 – What market are you serving? This is your ideal client.

2 – For this ideal client you should answer the following:
What defines success for them?
What questions will they have?
What are they struggling with?
What do you want them to do?

The answers to these questions will suggest how your brand is particularly suited to solve their problems and it will also suggest how you'll begin talking to those people with your branding.

Never forget that you're a designer, and creative problem solving is at the heart of what you do best. Put that to use in crafting a brand that uniquely speaks to what you do well.

Then get to work on that logo.

Additional Tools and Resources:
For full list, see: http://thirtybyforty.com/sign-up

Architect + Entrepreneur Startup Toolkit : Branding tools, resources, checklists, business card template, logo sample & icon pack. Download: *http://thirtybyforty.com/spl*

SWOT Analysis (Strengths, Weaknesses, Opportunities, Threats) http://en.wikipedia.org/wiki/SWOT_analysis

IGOR:

www.igorinternational.com/process/naming-guide-product-company-names.php

Graphics Software: (See Chapter 12)

    Photoshop
    Inkscape
    Pixlr
    Pixelmator
    GIMP
    Canva

Logo Design:

    99Designs.com
    Fiverr.com
    HipsterLogoGenerator.com
    You!

Business cards:

    Over-night Prints.com
    Zazzle.com

4 | Marketing

"Eighty percent of success is showing up."
- Woody Allen

Now that you've defined your ideal client and developed a basic brand message, it's time to take your brand to the world. Marketing your design practice is a job that's never finished; your sustained effort in the early days is required just to get noticed.

With marketing, as with many things, the easy thing to do isn't necessarily the right thing to do. You might consider setting up your dream studio as priority number one. Rent a highly visible office space; order new furniture, computers and plotters, and acquire all the trappings that define a real business to you.

You must not fall for this trap.

Those things will come when you have work to do (or even later). The most pressing task you face now is called business development. You need work. You need to take the brand you've been developing, announce your presence to the world and start filling your boards with projects. Without projects your business doesn't exist.

Marketing probably isn't something you've had much experience with as an employee. It's certainly nothing I was ever taught in architecture school. If your office experience was like mine, projects were probably passed to you as your schedule allowed. This all changes when you're a business owner. You'll devote a lot of time to marketing — not only to get the right projects but also to make sure your brand is delivering on the promises you've made.

At its core the goal of marketing is to let people (your target market) know what you do (your unique selling proposition, or USP) and how you do it (your narrative).

Once you've put been in business for a while and completed a few projects of your own, you'll come to understand that marketing actually extends far beyond these early steps, touching almost every aspect of the way you run your business. From keeping clients happy and projects running smoothly to writing e-mails and contract agreements; it's all marketing. You want to be sure your clients, your project team, contractors, consultants and collaborators all have a positive, professional experience with your brand. Ideally, you want that experience to warrant a recommendation to others.

Target market. This builds on work you completed in the previous chapter. Begin by clearly defining exactly whom you'll be selling your products and services to. Make their avatar your ideal client. The more specifically you define this early on, the more successful you'll be in reaching them. Your limited marketing budget needs to be highly focused to be successful. Architects and designers aren't often taught marketing skills because our professional training has yet to realize its value. Take a little time to educate yourself by reading online, watching YouTube videos, or audit an iTunes University course. Understand the basic theory, because you'll need a working lexicon.

As a starting point, magazines are a great resource. Think about the group of people who subscribe to and read Architectural Digest (ultra-expensive, formal architecture). They're much different from the group who reads Dwell Magazine. Each publication's branding and marketing is aimed at a very specific market. In your business, you decide whom you'd rather work with – the ones who read Dwell or the ones who read AD.

Look closely at the advertisements in each magazine; they're a great resource for divining what each market values. You're more likely to see a Big Ass Fans ad than a Tiffany's ad in Dwell. Look at the photographs, the styling and the captions. Each one says a little about the things each demographic value most. Figure out what your ideal client values, what they desire, where they hang out, what they read, where they vacation, what their family looks like, what they do in their spare time and what kind of music they listen to. If you were to look in their pockets, what would you find?

Craft your brand to attract these people, and design your marketing strategy to appeal to their sensibilities.

Action Items: Develop your target market avatar to represent your desired clients; be as detailed as you can in describing them. List every possible location they might frequent: web, blogs, community, print, forums (online and off), social clubs, day care centers, etc. If you're not already familiar with them, research the four C's (consumer, cost, communication, convenience), the four P's (product, price, promotion, place), and foundational marketing theory.

Your USP. What's a USP you say? It's your unique selling proposition (or point depending on whom you ask). It's a term developed by Rosser Reeves of Ted Bates & Company - one of the largest ad agencies in the world. Simply stated your USP is that which differentiates you in the marketplace. Your USP defines what makes you a better value than the other choices available. One of the reasons that 80 percent of new businesses fail in the first 18 months is their unwillingness to define their USP.

If you're struggling to define your USP, there are many resources available (like this chart: mightywisemedia.com/media/VP-Canvas-Triggers_B1.pdf). Although historically much of a designer or an architect's work has been local, the Internet has opened access to the world -- you'll be competing in a global marketplace. To stand out you'll have to differentiate.

Many in the entrepreneurial world refer to differentiation as, "niching down." Get specific. Can you simply state how you're different from your competitors? Is it your experience in a certain field? Do you know green roofs like no one else? Do you understand how to carefully manage construction waste to save your client money on the back end? Do you have specialized knowledge related to high performance building skins?

Part of defining your USP is determining precisely what your niche will be. Some architects are generalists, while others are highly focused and work on a singular project type. When you're just starting out I think it's more challenging to build a general practice. Of course, if you're purchasing or inheriting one, that's different. To be a "jack-of-all-trades" is to be "a master of none." Trying to serve everyone dilutes your brand message and will ultimately short-circuit your success.

The more distinguished your service, the better chance you have of becoming the definitive resource in your field. This is niching-down. Cultivate a set of skills valued by a select group of clients looking for a specific service. Passivhaus designers are experiencing strong, niche-specific growth currently, but there are many others to consider. Competitors in your area may be doing this very thing, but you may fill a need they aren't or go online, where they aren't present.

A niche-specific approach isn't without risk. Specializing in one thing means that when the market inevitably softens, all your business will go with it. Investing your efforts into related niches (green roofs for high end homes vs. large-scale commercial projects) will protect against this to some degree, but again you'll have to balance the dilution of your brand's identity. Building passive income streams can buffer the soft spots and bolster your message. Choose carefully and always remember that your business is your brand; make sure it's the kind of work you want to be doing.

You may be passionate about doing vegetated roofs right now, but five years from now you'll be known as the person who does really great vegetated roofs. Envisioning the daily business operations at a point in the future (five or even 10 years from now) is a good way of charting a course of action today. The work that you do today is the work you will get tomorrow. Make certain that future day is one you'll want to show up for in your business.

Action Items: Articulate your USP and define your target niche(s). Write it down and keep it visible in your workspace. This way you won't forget what you're seeking to do and who you're seeking to help.

Origin Story and Narrative. We discussed this concept in the previous chapter on branding but it bears repeating. When given a choice between something that has a back story, a narrative, and something that doesn't, people will usually choose the one with the story.

Brian Preston founded Lamon Luther (lamonluther.com), a Georgia furniture company, as a "tribute to a dying generation of craftsmen." The company hires carpenters who have fallen on hard times – some recently jailed, others having lost their jobs and their homes – to design and make hand-crafted, unique items in their local furniture shop to be sold worldwide. It's more than just a business, it reasserts the value of craft, exudes ingenuity, and it gives people in desperate need of another chance in life an opportunity to be part of something larger than themselves.

I stumbled across their company more than a year ago. I liked their story so much that I signed up for their e-mail list and I never forgot about them. It was their story that I remembered. Not their breadboards or their tables – although they're really beautiful – the story made an emotional connection. And, the next time I need a breadboard, I know exactly where I'll be buying it.

Your brand should strive for this kind of resonance when developing a narrative. Think about how you can make it something people will remember a year from now. Make it compelling, make it interesting, and provoke someone's inner passion. Memorable stories are easy to market.

Now it's your turn. What's your story? It should dovetail with the branding exercises from the previous chapter. It doesn't have to be long or involve feeding the hungry; it just has to be genuine and factual.

If you're just starting out and don't have a large body of work to draw on and support your story, you still have a story to tell. How did you come to be a designer or an architect or a furniture maker? What landed you where you are today? Where did you grow up? What's the one thing you know better than anyone? Don't think of it as a final draft; it's a first draft. Revise it and refine it as you build your business; you only need a place to start.

Your portfolio of constructed projects and previous clients can unlock many doors. Without them, building your own practice will be difficult. Think about what this means to a potential client. You're asking them to assume all of the risk without understanding any of the benefits. If you can't prove to a new client that someone has trusted you and you've executed on that trust before, it's going to be a tough sell.

Beyond the physical manifestation of your abilities, you need a set of skills to sell. The only two ways that I know of to build those skills are time and experience. Ideally, you want the development of those skills to be paid for by someone else and under the direction of another skilled professional. Someone whose work you respect and admire.

If you don't have a portfolio of work, you might not be ready for traditional practice. But it also shouldn't keep you from taking a more entrepreneurial approach to your business. I think working for someone else; being an employee is a good experience, at least for a while. Participate in the process of building; create something standing out there in the world. Work for someone who knows the business of architecture, study client behaviors, make connections in the field, and figure out how a building really goes together. Most importantly, make mistakes. You're guaranteed to learn from them and it will be in a place that's sheltered from the immediate financial (and legal) consequences that practicing on your own can invite.

If you're fortunate enough to have an established portfolio of work, make sure you've documented it with high-quality photographs and presentation drawings. There's nothing like the real thing to sell your talents to a client. Don't let poor photography obstruct the message. Photo shoots are expensive ($2,500 – $5,000+ per day) so initially you may opt to purchase a good digital SLR camera (a deductible expense) and take the photos yourself. Presentation drawings are easy to complete in the early days of your business before you have much work on your boards.

Built work is invaluable; it constitutes a substantial time and financial investment and clients recognize its value. That's what will net you more work and the opportunity for publication online and in print. Choose visuals that uniquely tell your viewpoint.

If you're coming from an established firm with several projects in the vault, you'll want to secure the necessary rights to use them in your own marketing materials.

What works for me: I had many projects that had been professionally photographed from previous employers. Only a few of those were ones I wanted to use for my own marketing purposes because only a few told the story I wanted to tell. I contacted the photographers and each asked that I provide a letter from my previous employer (who paid for the photo shoot) stating that I was involved in the subject projects. As you might imagine, my previous employer wasn't exactly excited about this prospect, but they did provide a letter saying that I worked on them which was enough to allow me to purchase use rights from several photographers.

You'll want to clarify the usage terms before you purchase. I was allowed to use their photographs on my website and in promotional materials that I created, but nothing in print, online magazines, or publications. The cost of this varied based on the photographer but it generally ranged from $175-300 for usage rights.

I also bolstered these professional photos with ones I had been taking with my digital SLR. While working for others, I always tried to document and archive the projects I worked on as they were completed knowing that one day I might need them. The professional photos are far better than mine and it's a professional service I now budget for in my business.

Action Items: Commit your story to words and gather the visual materials to support it.

Website. Now that you have the portfolio pulled together, you need a plan to get it in front of your ideal clients, your target market. You want to be visible to your potential clients wherever they spend time. For your lean-startup business, that means online.

You'll likely have little money to spend on paid advertising and I would advise against it anyway. Paid advertising in magazines is expensive because it requires constant cash inputs. An ad run for a single month may cost you $2500 or more (depending on the size, placement, magazine circulation, etc.) and that's for a onetime (potential) viewing. For print ads to be successful they need to be part of a longer campaign. You can't just pay for a month and expect it to net all the work you need for the next quarter or two. Besides, there are better ways to broadcast your brand message.

Your website is without question the single most effective marketing strategy for business development today. Fortunately, it's also very affordable. As far as marketing tools go, your website is an inexpensive and invaluable marketing tool that your business can't live without.

Think of your business as a giant wheel. At the center of that wheel is your website. Everything else in the world should point back to your website. Each spoke is a link directing prospective clients back to your property. A web address is one of the most valuable purchases you can make today and that's true for any business. Develop this piece of online real estate the way you would a project, invest your design skills and use it as a testing platform to hone your marketing message.

But make sure it's your own. Sites like Houzz.com allow you to build not only your profile but also a website for free. The site designer on Houzz is easy to use and the resulting site they automatically create for you is visually strong; it's a good start. However, building a site on Houzz.com actually helps them more than it helps you because they have the SEO skills to put your images and backlinks to work for them. Choosing their platform to promote your business will actually undermine your own efforts to rank in Google in the future.

It's already happening today, Houzz is outranking almost everyone in the design field for search terms in Google related to architecture, interior design, and construction. Don't let them outrank you for your business name too.

Owning your website means you'll have full control over everything. Control over the aesthetics, hosting, content management and monetization. It's an asset. Like anything else you own, you'll also own the responsibility for fixing it when it breaks.

If you've never built a website before it's a relatively simple process to dive into. Here are the basic steps:

> 1 – **Choose a web host.** I use Bluehost.com but there are many others. Bluehost offers a nice balance of responsive customer service and reliability. You can research hosting companies for more details and reviews. Check to make sure they offer a one-click WordPress installation. WordPress is a content management system (CMS) which is the free software that the vast majority of the world uses to construct websites. I recommend you use it to build your site too.
>
> *NOTE: Don't confuse WordPress.org (the CMS) and WordPress.com (the host). WordPress.com is a host, very similar to the Google's Blogger host (blogspot.com). Many people use this as a free way to begin blogging, but you want to self-host your website not use someone else's domain name.*

When you select hosting you'll need to pay for the first year (or two or three) all at once. You may see a hosting offer for $3.95/month, but you'll need to multiply that by 12 to get the annual cost, the longer the term the less expensive it is.

2 – **Register a domain name.** This should be your business name ending in .com or .net format, for example, Designlab.com. I didn't register all forms of my business name just to save a little, but that's up to you. Many people purchase all forms (.com, .net, .biz, etc.) and set up a redirect for everything other than the .com format. This is the equivalent of more spokes on the wheel pointing back to the .com site, your central domain. This way when someone enters Designlab.net into the search bar it takes him or her to Designlab.com. You can register domain names for as little as $0.99 cents for the first year – Google is your friend. Thereafter you'll pay about $15/year per domain to maintain the registration.

3 – **Install WordPress.** After you've purchased the domain, you need to install WordPress to use your location on the Internet. WordPress is free software, it's a type of CMS – a content management system. You can think of it like an operating system that allows you to easily post and update your content on the web – photos, blog posts, and an infinite number of pages. Web hosts make this an easy process and most have a simple wizard to walk you through the setup. With Bluehost, it's literally one click and you're done.

4 – **Install Your WordPress Theme.** A theme determines the look and feel of your site and there are tens of thousands of themes to choose from. Sites like Themeforest.net and WooThemes.com are good starting points. Free options are available too, but recognize that you may look like everyone else if you use a free template. Spend $50-100 on a designed theme that fits your brand aesthetic. Make sure the theme you buy is 'Responsive,' meaning that it will readjust its formatting to the screen resolution of the device reading it. Mobile traffic constitutes an increasing share of web visits and if your site doesn't adjust it to a phone's screen size your lead may leave your site in a few seconds.

5 – **Install Plug-ins.** At the risk of diving too deep, thousands of plug-ins exist that can extend the functionality of your WordPress site. They range from

shopping carts, to backups, to landing pages and Instagram viewers. You should investigate these as you dive deeper into WordPress.

The one plug-in you absolutely need to install initially is **WordPress SEO** by Yoast. This plug-in will point out the elements of your site that affect search engine ranking – which is ultimately how your clients will find you. There are helpful wizards to walk you through the factors you'll need to add to each post and page as well as a handy tool for adding your **Google Analytics** tracking code without having to know how to code.

Google Analytics uses a unique code that's embedded on your website to track the traffic coming to and from your website. Knowing where and how much traffic is coming can help hone your message and develop content based on the keywords people are typing into Google to arrive at your site. It's tied to a Gmail address (you do have a Gmail address, right?) and the dashboard is accessed through a web portal. You can always Google it for more information and video tutorials will guide you through the process of setting it up.

If all this sounds too complicated, there are plug-and-play options as well. Sites like Squarespace.com offer prepackaged solutions, similar to the Houzz site designer. Aesthetically, Squarespace offers a wider range of themes to choose from, but you'll pay between $8-30 per month for the convenience. The real advantage here is that you don't need to sign up for separate hosting or worry about installing anything to get started. It's not as flexible as WordPress, but it's quite simple.

The One Thing. It's easy to get caught up in the look and feel of your site. It should reinforce your brand certainly, but think beyond aesthetics for a moment and ask yourself this question, "What's the one thing I want someone visiting my site to do?" Your home page should answer this question.

Some 'One Thing' examples to consider:

1- Contact you (Skype, Call, E-mail, etc.) – for a paid (or free) initial consultation, to discuss their project.

2 - Sign up for your e-mail list. An Internet marketing trick we'll discuss in Chapter 5. This is an exchange of someone's e-mail for a specific offer or "lead-magnet."

3 – Enter your client prequalification funnel; an automated series of steps that determines whether the prospective client is a good fit before you ever meet.

4 – Buy a product you sell. This can be floor plan sets, productized service packages (design or consultation), a site visit, furniture, objects; whatever you decide.

5 – Communicate a story. Make the story about the visitor, not you. Help him or her understand what your brand does and how it can help them.

When someone visits the home page is it clear what you're expecting him or her to do? Too often architects and designers focus on the visuals and describe the images with elitist terms. Use accessible language to tell your story and you'll establish a point of distinction that visitors will appreciate. No one likes to feel uneducated and design can be intimidating to the uninitiated. Making someone feel accepted while educating them will go a long way towards them taking the first step to contact you and discuss their project.

If your site isn't saying one thing, work on it until it is. One way to test this objectively is to have someone else look at it. I use an online tool called Peek (peek.usertesting.com) which crowdsources web users to record a five-minute video of them surfing your site. You simply enter your URL in their web interface and a few hours later you receive an e-mail with a link to a random web user using your site. In the video they describe what kind of site they think it is and what their likely next actions are when visiting it. They will often make suggestions on improvements or tweaks to make it better. The free tool is limited to 3 five-minute video requests per month, which should be more than enough to do some basic testing and fine tuning.

What works for me: Website development was a skill I wanted to learn so I simply followed an online tutorial for setting up a WordPress website. I purchased the domain through Bluehost and a professionally designed theme from Themeforest and slowly picked my way through the setup process.

A word of caution: resist the urge to spend hour after hour tweaking your website. I did and despite my warning you probably will too. We're aesthetic individuals. It's hard not to look at something that could be improved and not want to improve it. There's always that one additional thing to adjust in the sidebar, or a header logo that needs to be larger. Your website needs to be functional, but turning it into a magnum opus is misdirected energy. Instead, spend the time getting it in front of your target market. Build the spokes to the center of the wheel.

You can do this by guest posting on other blogs, by participating in design discussions online, by being an active professional on Houzz.com and creating content on your own website. All these actions will net you the fuel for your business – paying clients.

Action Items: Purchase the domain name that correlates with your business name. Set up your hosting account, install a theme and begin building your online presence with the story, text and visuals you gathered in the previous step. Make sure your home page is saying 'One Thing' and no more.

Once you've put your website together, you can refer prospective clients and contacts to it. This is your virtual studio. Now let people know where it is. There's a deep well of website strategies that you'll dig into in the future as you gain confidence using WordPress, for now, establishing your site is an excellent first step.

3C's. Here's a primer on the foundational marketing theory called the three C's. It's essentially a Venn diagram with three circles. One circle is your Customer, one is your Competition, and the third is your Company. Where these circles overlap is your marketing strategy. It's what your customer's want, your competitor's weakness and the thing your company is offering.

> **Company.** What is your company good at? What do you want to do? What are your resources?
>
> **Customers.** Who is your ideal customer? What are their needs? How do they purchase?
>
> **Competition.** What are their weak spots? What aren't they offering that you could? How do they sell?

The intersection of what you do best, what the consumer wants most and what your competition struggles to provide is your unique selling proposition; that's the place you own in the market. When you find this sweet spot and build your marketing around it, your services will sell themselves.

Leads. Work can come from many sources. You'll need to rely heavily on personal and professional networks both online and off. Early projects may come from family and friends or your own need for a home. Be sure everyone in your network knows what you're doing and the kind of work you're seeking.

Here are some marketing channels available to you:

> **Professional networks:** realtors, contractors, bankers and anyone involved in the building pipeline.
>
> **Personal networks:** family and friends.
>
> **Paid advertising:** Google AdWords, print (magazines, newspaper).
>
> **Directory listings:** Behance, design directories.
>
> **Publications:** magazines (online and print).
>
> **Design Competitions:** check Archdaily, Death By Architecture, or Bustler.
>
> **Pro bono work:** can lead to paying jobs.
>
> **Writing:** develops a lifelong skill and positions you as the expert.
>
> **Social media:** Facebook, Pinterest, Houzz, Twitter.
>
> **YouTube or Vimeo:** these are powerful search engines.

If you've been diligent about defining exactly what your brand is that will guide the best marketing strategy to pursue. It's unlikely you'll net many commercial development jobs by marketing on Pinterest or Facebook. But you may find that a pro-bono nursery school addition nets some residential work from growing young families.

You have more time than money right now; leverage that resource however you can.

What works for me: With the benefit of hindsight I can say there were a few keys to my marketing successes.

> **1- Skill set.** Marketing is time intensive and difficult work. Marketing without a set of skills to market is nearly impossible. The fundamentals of marketing rely on supply and demand, make sure your skill set can generate demand and you'll find more opportunity.

Before starting my business, I set out to work for award-winning design firms. Naturally, I would have a better chance to work on award-winning projects in those kinds of firms. I would also be able to learn the process of putting those projects together, understand how the clients were won, what the design process looked like, how they billed, how they marketed, how they resolved problems, etc. By the time I was ready to leave and open my own firm; I had designed several award-winning projects and had been intimately involved in every aspect of the operations of a successful firm. The plan worked.

If this is a goal of yours, then I strongly encourage you to work for people whose work you admire. This one thing, above all others, is crucially important to you gaining traction in the world. You'll learn the project delivery process from a group of professionals used to generating high-quality work. You'll gain the experience of designing projects, meeting with clients, drafting proposals, and mediating problems onsite and in the office.

My experience doing this also taught me some things that I didn't want to emulate. I could see opportunities for things I could improve upon. Working for others is conducting surveillance on your future competitors - market research. It's an investment in yourself and that's something that you can take with you wherever you go.

2 – **Network**. My first big break after opening my firm came from the recommendation of a builder I had worked with previously. I made sure I always over delivered at every step. If I told them it would take two weeks; I delivered it in a week. If I told them it would cost X, I would always come in under X. When they e-mailed, I e-mailed back in fewer than 24 hours. I met every deadline and I gave them my best work. That client has continued to do several projects each year, from the very small to the very large and when they need something they call me. I made the choice an easy one for them because they look good when things progress as planned, ahead of schedule and under budget.

I also rely on referrals from past clients, friends, realtors and other architects. Be nice, be helpful and you'll get the referral without even having to ask.

3 – **Built work**. This refers, in part, back to the first strategy that worked for me. Working for an award-

winning firm means you'll have a better chance of stacking your portfolio with award-winning projects and the title of 'award-winning architect.' Building a portfolio of built-work is invaluable. But, when you're working for someone else, they get the real credit, not you.

There are ways around this. Hire yourself. I turned the need for a home for my family into a design opportunity and I did it while I had the financial security of full-time employment. When it was done I entered it into as many competitions as possible, took photos, and publicized it. Although it didn't win any awards, it was a finalist in a Dwell Homes competition and it's been featured in a book on small houses.

Now when I meet prospective clients (in my home), they can see firsthand what I'm able to do. Recognize that this can be a disadvantage too. If the kind of home you design for yourself differs from the kind of home your target market is looking for, they may find it hard to look past. Now that my business is growing, I'm constructing a separate studio on my property dedicated solely to my business and it's another chance to hire myself.

4 – Houzz.com. One part professional directory, one part image-based search engine, Houzz has serious market share in the home design industry. I've written an entire book on the ways I use Houzz to market to clients (The Unofficial Guide to Houzz.com). I've had great success with the techniques I describe in the book. I have a strategy for using Houzz to specifically target leads which has resulted in many projects for my business.

5 – Online. I've tried many things online to stand out from my competition. This is one of the easiest places to be different. Social media can be a huge time suck if you let it. It's impossible to consistently post everywhere with some regularity. You have a blog for your website, a Facebook page, a Pinterest account, Houzz, Architizer, Twitter, YouTube, and on and on. Find one or two that work for you and invest in those. In my opinion, the biggest points of traction for architects and designers are: Houzz, Pinterest, YouTube, and Facebook. But this depends on the kind of clients you're seeking. I focus on residential design so these channels are used by my clients the most. So far, only Houzz has delivered paying clients to my business.

Now it's your turn. Finding the right mix of marketing techniques will take some experimentation. Just thinking about marketing your products and services is an exercise that will force you to view your business in a new light. What makes you buy something when you're out shopping? What can you do to trigger that impulse? How can you answer the questions people will invariably have about what you do? Generate the FAQ for your business and use that as a marketing plan – talk about the process, the cost, the schedule, what happens when problems arise.

This is an iterative process rather than a strictly systematized, step-by-step sequence. You'll develop a basic version of what you have to offer at first, something with a stripped-down feature set, and offer it for sale via one of the many channels above. It's really the market that will determine whether people will think your USP is valuable. If people aren't buying what you're selling, set aside your ego, accept it and pivot.

The very definition of insanity is doing the same thing over and over and expecting a different result. A failure gives you something valuable: information. Learn from it, refine, iterate and pivot to something new, test and retest. Marketing is a perpetual exercise — you'll always be seeking new work.

Action Items: Start marketing. You first have to cast a net to see what kind of life is out there. Pick something; begin testing ideas to see what works and what doesn't. Call friends, family, stop by a local realtor's office, offer something for free, write an article for your local paper, enter a competition – get out there and make something happen.

Get started:

- Complete your professional and business social media profiles and begin curating the content on each of those platforms. I recommend starting with your Houzz.com profile. Build each one out to a point where they can reliably refer business to your website.

- Broadcast what you're doing to your network: contractors, realtors, consultants, colleagues, friends and family.

- Keep building your online presence, your website is the center of the wheel, build the spokes back to it.

5 | Internet Marketing

"Chaos was the law of nature; order was the dream of man."
— Henry Adams

The Internet has opened the doors for architects and designers to practice globally. You can create a business that you can take with you anywhere you choose to live in the world. This freedom is made possible by the Internet. No longer are we constrained to practice in our local neighborhood.

Print marketing, brochures, and direct mail are vestiges of an old economy. Today, they're practically irrelevant. It's good news for the lean start-up, because you can compete against established firms online. Once you've built your website, you need a working knowledge of Internet marketing principles to give your business a competitive edge. Although Internet marketers have an auspicious reputation, we can learn from their practices and apply them to our trade.

Marketing takes many forms online, but the basic categories of Internet marketing are:

Advertising. We're confronted with ads everywhere in our lives, but the number of ads we're exposed to online is exponentially greater than anywhere else. We see so many that we've developed natural blinders to help us look past the clutter of the ads so we can focus on the information we're searching for. As a response to this, Internet marketers have been forced to deploy more ninja-like tricks to refocus our attention on their ads. They understand that the more relevant an ad is to what we're searching for, the more likely we are to click on it. And clicks translate into revenue for the company selling the ad.

If you've ever searched for an item to purchase online, chances are good you've been the target of contextual ads and a remarketing campaign. Search for boots, sunglasses, software, or a laptop and you'll immediately begin to see "promoted options" served to you as search results. As you click on search results, visit vendors and view products, a stealthy marketing campaign is observing your behavior. They know what you've added to your shopping cart, how many pages you've visited, where exactly on those pages you've clicked and what you've spent the most time viewing.

If you depart without buying anything, you'll be stalked by images of the exact products that you studied. As you surf the Internet over the next week, the ads you see were purchased by the company whose website you visited and queried. That company paid an advertising network to push ads to your computer based on your browsing behavior on their site. You may have visited six pages, or added an item to the shopping cart or filled out a form. These actions automatically set their marketing campaign in motion and their most successful, highly converting ads were shown to you in hopes of swaying you to buy their product, right then.

If you clicked on one of those ads, you "converted." In Internet marketing parlance, a conversion happens each time you take an intended action. A conversion on an ad means a click through to the ad purchaser's website. Again, you convert when you turn from a lead (a visitor on the website) into a sale (you buy something). The reason you saw the ads we just spoke about is that remarketing converts 300-400% higher than standard paid ads. That means you're three to four times as likely to click on an ad for an item that previously interested you than you are on a random product.

Let's say I'm searching for "men's boots" in Google. Among the search results I'm shown a paid ad for L.L. Bean duck boots. What I was *actually* looking for was black Doc Martens. Even though I saw the ad for the duck boots (marketers call this an impression), it wasn't relevant to what I was really seeking. L.L. Bean paid for the impression even though it was wasted on me.

If you're a company paying for ads based on the number of impressions, you want the ads to be contextual – meaning they're shown only when a customer searches for men's boots. But the most valuable time for the ad to show up is when the customer is ready to buy. For example, when he or she has added a pair of boots to a shopping cart that look like the boots you sell. They've shown their intent that they're ready to buy; that's a very valuable impression. That's why you see so many remarketing ads after you've visited a store and added an item to your shopping cart. Even if you purchased the item already and you're no longer in the market for boots.

We're obviously not in the business of selling boots, so what can architects and designers learn from the Internet marketing ninjas? Make your message contextual everywhere. This means as you develop the content of your website: the 'About' page, the 'Blog', the 'Home' page. The real value of your online presence to a visitor is how well you curate the information a visitor sees. Think about the context of everything you publish.

Your home page should direct a new visitor through a logical sequence of actions. When someone arrives on your site, what do you want them to do (remember, one thing)? You probably want them to see some of your work; you want them to know what it costs to work with you, and how much it costs to build in your area. You'll want to tell them what's included in your service and what isn't. You'll want them to understand the way you prefer to work with clients. Think about the questions your clients may have when they arrive on your site. Answer those questions by walking them through a logically arranged sequence of information.

You're not buying ads or impressions, but you're linking the information on your site contextually. Your page describing the costs of working with an architect can link out to a post about programming or ways to save money during the design process. Your page about what's included can link out to other consultant's websites that you work with or a typical fee breakdown. The natural evolution of this descriptive process of curation creates an information-rich web of interrelated information and helps Google index and rank your site.

Affiliate marketing. The next category of online marketing has a particularly notorious reputation. The underlying concept of affiliate marketing is commission-based referral. Affiliates recommend products: information products, software, tools, and courses to others in exchange for a commission from the product developer. In the early days of the Internet info-products were sold on affiliate networks. Many were structured as MLM (multi-level marketing) schemes and were often short courses on how to make money online. And the means for making money online? Affiliate marketing! How meta, right? But those days are, for the most part, behind us.

Here's how it works today. You promote products to your audience in exchange for a commission. Search for products being sold online that are specifically relevant the market you serve. Usually if the company has an affiliate program there's a link in their website footer that says, "Affiliates." If they do, you'll need to apply and be accepted into the program. This is usually a pro-forma process and it requires that you provide the URL to your website as proof of your ability to actively promote their products online.

As an affiliate, you earn a commission when a consumer completes a purchase after clicking on your embedded affiliate link. To generate these links, most companies offer an affiliate dashboard to select products and create affiliate links. These links each have your referrer's ID embedded, this is what you'll use to promote the products. Having generated the unique link, the next step is to create the content on your own website to pitch the product and finally you'll promote the content with the embedded link(s).

As someone visits your site, reads your helpful article and clicks on your affiliate link they're taken to the product page on the affiliated website. When they buy the product you receive a commission on the sale according to the terms of your affiliate agreement. It sounds like a lot of work to set up, but once established you don't have to do anything but promote the products on your website. Assuming you've crafted useful content for the consumer and only recommend products you believe in, it benefits you and the consumer.

If you do choose to promote products as an affiliate, make sure you disclose this fact either in the text of the blog post or on your website's Terms and Conditions.

So how much can you make? Typical commissions are 5 - 8.5% of the purchase price for many home product stores online. One popular choice and perhaps the simplest to join is the Amazon Associates program. Amazon has proved its place in e-commerce and holds a database with more credit card numbers than any company in the world. Consumers trust Amazon and with more and more home products available for sale it's an affiliate opportunity for architects and designers. They offer many interior accessories, hardware and even plumbing fixtures. Choose products that fit with your brand message and products that you know are high quality.

Amazon's affiliate program is special for a few reasons, one because it offers a 24-hour tracking cookie. This means that someone visiting Amazon from your affiliate link has 24-hours to make a purchase. Anything they purchase within that window will be attributed to you. Even better, the commission percentage you receive is calculated on the entire cart price. If someone purchases a $15 cabinet pull from your blog's affiliate link but they also buy a 50-inch flat screen TV for $849, your commission will be 5% of the total purchase price. That's a little more than $43 for the small task of creating an affiliate link.

If you live in a state that doesn't play well with Amazon, you're out of luck. As of 2015, residents in Arkansas, Colorado, Maine, Missouri, Rhode Island, and Vermont are ineligible for the program.

Affiliate programs can be found everywhere online. Search for the building or design products you specify as a routine part of your practice and you're bound to find an e-commerce platform selling it and an opportunity to become an affiliate.

Think about products consumers typically buy and install themselves like: faucets, lighting fixtures, appliances, hardware and accessories. The site, GreenAffiliatePrograms.net has a complete listing of affiliate programs to choose from in the green products industry.

Landing (Squeeze) Pages. When you think like an Internet marketer you begin to notice opportunity everywhere. Marketers approach the world with a singular focus – to generate income using the most efficient means. Architects and designers are usually concerned more with how their website looks rather than how well it functions or generates revenue. The landing, or squeeze page is your chance to think like a marketer and still maintain an aesthetically pleasing web page.

What is it? It's essentially a web page where the viewer is directed to do only one thing. The Internet marketer knows the exact value of a customer and their value is tied to their e-mail. The larger your e-mail list, the more valuable it is. The goal of the landing page is to capture a visitor's e-mail address and it has a very clear message, "Enter your e-mail to receive _____." The blank is filled in with what marketer's call a 'lead magnet.' Typically it's an e-mail newsletter (!), a checklist, a free report, or an e-book; anything of value. It's up to you to determine what the magnet is but it has to be attractive enough to warrant the viewer trading their e-mail address away for it. The landing page 'squeezes' a transaction, it forces an immediate exchange. You want the name and e-mail of the visitor and in return you're offering something useful.

E-mail marketing has been used by Internet marketers for many years because it works. It's a way to reach out and intimately engage with an audience. If you've been monitoring your website traffic via your analytics, you know that the number of page loads and unique visitors are a measure of how successful you've been at driving search traffic to your site. The analytics allow you to see their behavior when they visit, how long they stay, what they click on, where they go to when they're done. But analytics offer so much information it can be overwhelming and difficult to make sense of. Fundamentally, those numbers in your dashboard are people.

As a business owner the most important thing for you to figure out is which of the many visitors that land on your site are most engaged with what you have to offer. Who is connecting with your brand message? A landing page allows you to collect the e-mails of those people and it transforms the relationship between you and them. It changes an abstract number in your analytics into a person with a name and e-mail address.

You can appreciate now how important it is to offer a lead magnet that's aligned with the thing or things that you do particularly well. When the two correspond, the e-mails you capture will be especially relevant because they've shown interest in the lead magnet and it was valuable enough for them to offer you the chance to communicate with them by e-mail.

An e-mail list is a business asset that you control, it's your property and it has an assignable dollar value. Companies buy access to targeted e-mail lists and in business, control is everything.

The list is another spoke in the hub analogy we discussed earlier but it's a special one. This spoke can be used to point at whatever center you choose. The center hub could be a store, a resource page with affiliate links, a book, software, designs, a furniture line, a lecture series, a course, or a special promotion.

Building an engaged e-mail list is like having your own army of forces you can summon at will. These are your biggest fans and they'll be treated with special care. Give them early notification of promotions, or exclusive access to product releases – perhaps it's your own hardware line or desk accessories or laser-cut iPad cases.

Now that you have an e-mail list what do you do with it? The first rule is to keep in touch. If the only effort you make to contact your list is when you have something to sell how do you think they'll react? How would you react? Poorly, right? If you keep in touch, let's say monthly, and always offer something valuable; when it's time to promote something for sale to your list they'll be much more likely to respond positively and support you.

What's valuable? That's up to you to decide. Please don't make it a 'newsletter,' though. I can't think of anything more unimaginative than a 'newsletter." Your offering is a chance for you to be creative. Tell a story about a recent project and a lesson learned. Send a sketch of what you're designing. Send an Instagram thumbnail. How about a link to a book you just finished?

Think about the e-mails you always open and the ones you consistently delete. Can you discern any particular pattern? The ones I always open are: well-designed, they offer something I can't get elsewhere (exclusivity), they're usually very short and they typically include an image or two.

Here are a few other ideas to consider:

> - A photo of a current project in design or construction – just one. Link it back to your website and a blog post where they can read more.
>
> - Link to a relevant article with a few clever words.
>
> - New product recommendation or review by you (make it a linked image).
>
> - Simple quote, with a link embedded to expand on it.

If you make it simple and memorable, people will look forward to your monthly (or quarterly) e-mail, open it and engage with it rather than dreading yet another 'newsletter' or large block of text they'll never read.

What works for me: I use MailChimp as my e-mail marketing service provider. Because my list is still below the subscriber threshold of two-thousand, I'm enrolled in the 'Forever Free' program. If you'd like to see exactly how I use e-mail in my marketing funnel, be sure to subscribe to my list. You'll find it at: http://thirtybyforty.com.

Autoresponders. You can adopt another tool from the Internet marketing world to automate the chore of e-mailing. It's called an autoresponder. An autoresponder, as the name implies, automatically responds to a trigger event by sending an e-mail or series of e-mails to the new subscriber. The trigger event in this case would be someone subscribing to your list.

When one enters and confirms an e-mail address in the form on your site, your e-mail service provider is notified and the autoresponder begins sending them e-mails at an interval of your choice. Each e-mail has been planned as a sequence and prewritten by you and can be delivered over a period of weeks or months. It should be designed to tell a story or walk your subscriber through a process – moving them from point A to point B.

An often-quoted statistic in the marketing world says that it typically takes seven points of contact with a potential client before they'll feel comfortable enough to hire you. An autoresponder can give you as many points of contact as you'd like. With each successive e-mail, your subscriber will know you a little better and you have a chance to prove your value to them. Draft the e-mail series once and the autoresponder handles the delivery for you, freeing you to do other things that matter to you and for the business.

Autoresponders are offered by most e-mail marketing service providers. It's an upgraded feature so expect to pay a nominal monthly fee for access.

Providers: AWeber vs. MailChimp. Although there are many other services online, AWeber and MailChimp are two of the most popular with the online business start-up community. With respect to the paid plans, the two are similar. The user interface, helpful video tutorials, template designs and WordPress integration available through MailChimp make for a better overall experience. MailChimp also appeals to my design sensibilities more than AWeber, which feels clinical and has a reputation for a non-intuitive user interface. AWeber has the edge though when it comes to list analytics and understanding how your subscribers engage with the e-mails you send.

MailChimp has the advantage of being "Forever Free" compared with AWeber's $19 / month ($1 for your first month). Assuming your list has fewer than 2,000 subscribers, you send fewer than 12,000 e-mails per month (aggregate total) and you can live with their branding in the footer of your e-mails, MailChimp is a good place to start collecting e-mails.

Each service offers customization and import/export options which make moving from one to the other relatively easy. You can't go wrong with either option, but ease of set up is worth a lot if you're new to autoresponders and for that reason again I recommend MailChimp.

To access the autoresponder feature with either of these services, you'll need to upgrade to a monthly pricing structure. The two competitors are hard to directly compare on pricing, but MailChimp wins in the paid plan category when you have fewer than 1,000 subscribers and they're roughly equal above that threshold. Once you have more than 2,500 subscribers on your list, you should be monetizing your list (routinely offering something for sale), which should offset the nominal monthly cost of maintaining it.

Similarities:

- Customization. Hundreds of e-mail templates to choose from basic to advanced.
- Integration. Offers e-mail provider (Gmail) and application integration (WordPress)
- Tracking. Detailed information on user engagement and clicks on e-mails sent.
- Time Based. Choose when you send autoresponse e-mail campaigns.
- Event-based triggers. Certain autoresponses sent based on user behavior (open, purchase, click, etc.)
- List Segmentation. Ability to categorize and subdivide list based on parameters of your choosing.
- Unlimited sends per month.

Differences:
> **AWeber:**
>> $19 / month 0 – 500 subscribers
>>
>> $29 / month 501 – 2500 subscribers
>>
>> Less intuitive UI
>>
>> Robust analytics
>>
>> Advanced set up, difficult to fine tune without HTML knowledge
>
> **MailChimp:**
>> $10 / month 0 – 500 subscribers
>>
>> $15 / month 500 – 1000 subscribers
>>
>> $30 / month 1001 – 2500 subscribers
>>
>> Easy to set up and tweak with WYSIWYG interface

Content. The most important part of the autoresponder series is the content. Use it as an opportunity to deliver your brand message. Make it about your potential client; think about why they're coming to you and how you can help. Make the first e-mail an introduction; describe who you are and what you do informally. The idea is for them to connect to you as a person, give them a hook about what to expect in the second e-mail which could be, for example, about programming. In that e-mail you might include a link to a video describing your process for developing the program, tell them to expect another e-mail about budgeting soon. Follow-up with the next step in your process, break it down and walk them through the basics. Let them know how your process works, show them your sketches, reveal the messiness of design.

At this point you're building rapport with them and showing them that you're an expert. If you add a link to a "programming worksheet" in the e-mail, you'll be able to track who clicks the link in your analytics. If no one clicks it you'll know to pivot to something else and along the way discover what they consider valuable.

At the end of each e-mail offer a clear call-to-action. Tell them precisely what you want them to do: schedule a consultation, watch this video, purchase this training course, or get the book. Make each call-to-action a link; plain text is good, a clickable button is better.

SEO (Search Engine Optimization). This is the process of making the best use of the words and structure of your website for maximum visibility in the eyes of a search engine's crawling robots. If you're using WordPress, install the plug-in discussed in the previous chapter, **WordPress SEO** by Yoast. It will help you fine tune the SEO factors that matter for each page of your site.

It helps to have a basic understanding of SEO principles before you start loading your site with content.

1 - **Permalinks and URL structure.** Your page's URL (Uniform Resource Locator) is the web address. When you create pages on your website, you're generating a unique URL online. Google (and other search engines) use the title of this to understand what your page is about. You want the URLs you create to be keyword rich, not just a smattering of numbers and gibberish.

If I create a page on my site that describes the cost of working with an architect, the default URL permalink might be: http://thirtybyforty.com/p-01233 which doesn't tell the Google spiders anything about the post's content. By contrast, a URL that looks like this: http://thirtybyforty.com/cost-of-working-with-an-architect tells the spiders exactly what they need to know.

By default, WordPress isn't setup like this, you must go into your Dashboard > Settings > Permalink Settings and click on the button that says, "Post name." Each time you create a post or page make sure the title is SEO friendly as above and the URL will reflect this.

Google has said they weight the first three words in the title for search optimization. Your goal should be to put the keyword you're hoping to rank for in those first three words. As you build out your website with individual pages and posts, focus on creating posts and pages for as many keywords related to your field or niche as possible with your URL permalinks.

2 – **Keywords.** As a guideline, for each page or post try to make sure your keyword appears in the first 100 – 150 words of the text content too. This signals to the search engines that the ranking keyword correlates. The SEO plug-in by Yoast provides a keyword suggestion tool in each post or page

editor to help you figure out the terms people are searching for most frequently.

3 – **Tags**. Another indicator of content and hierarchy, tags are used to subdivide your article or page into coherent subtopics. If you use WordPress, the <h1> heading tag is automatically added to your post title. The remaining tags from <h2> to <h6> are for finer levels of resolution. Think of the <h2> as a subheading, <h3> is a deeper level subdivision and so on. No need to get carried away, simply organize your article logically for your reader (and Google).

4 – **Indexable Content**. Information, referred to as "content" by Internet marketers, is the meat of your site. The aggregate total of the words and images supporting those words is what Google uses to index and rank your site. Trends change, but currently the ideal content length according to Google is around 1,500 words per page or post. Google views very short content (fewer than 500 words) poorly while content much longer than 1,500 words has a lower chance of resonating with your visitors looking for easily digestible information.

Common sense would say that the content should only be as long as it takes to convey your message. Be smart; don't craft content just for the search engine's benefit. If you create information that's easy to consume and helpful to readers, you'll naturally start to see your traffic increase because visitors will share it and spend time reading it and engage with it. Google will see this and you'll benefit from it. That's the reason Google is always trying to improve their ranking factors to better discern what content users find valuable. If you get straight to the business of creating value, Google will eventually catch up.

Because a designer's website is full of images, understanding how a search engine indexes visual content is crucial to being discovered by clients searching for what you're offering. Provide alt-text for images, which tells search engines what's in the image. Provide a transcript for any video or audio content you create.

5 - **Outbound Links**. Indicating to Google the relevance of other pages on your site is the point of outbound links. This can mean sending the reader to other places online, but focus first on other relevant pages on your site.

To use our previous example, when we discuss the cost of working with an architect we have to include consultants, right? Why not create a page that describes all the parties who contribute to the design process? When you create the page build links to it. From this page you've created, build an outbound link back to the "cost" page and other relevant pages; maybe a "Resources" page which lists your preferred consultants and request a backlink from your consultant's web page.

When you do this repeatedly, Google understands how the pages on your site relate to each other and to the broader context of the Internet. The more information you can provide about relevancy the better chance you have at being ranked in organic search and the more your traffic will increase.

6 - **Multimedia.** Images convert very well, as do icons and buttons to click on. Diversify the content on your site for a better chance at capturing search traffic from a variety of sources (YouTube, Pinterest, Houzz, Instagram, and Facebook). Tell the search-engine spiders what's in the image by adding alt-text (see #4 above) and titles that clearly describe the content.

7 – **Page load speed.** Most people will wait approximately three seconds for a page to load. In fact, Amazon.com found that a 1 second difference in page loading speed costs them $1.6 billion a year. Small image sizes, streamlined CSS coding and your host all play a role in how fast your page loads. Experiment with online tools, like the MozBar plug-in and Google Webmaster Tools to discover where your page load speed can be optimized.

8 – **Social sharing.** If you create great things, you might as well make them easy to share on social networks. Adding social sharing buttons to your site not only helps build social proof for your brand but it's becoming an increasingly important ranking factor in Google's algorithm. I use the Simple Share Buttons Adder plug-in for WordPress because it's visually minimal.

9 – **Bounce rate.** The percentage of people who arrive at your site and leave without visiting another page is your bounce rate. A low number signals to Google that you've built a high-quality site that engages users and gives them a reason to stick (and click) around. Build internal links, write compelling copy and provide a clear message to your visitors. Objectively visit each page of your website and ask yourself, "Is it clear what I expect the user to do here?" Direct the user experience with

an obvious call to action. Use phrases like, "New here? Start here," to guide them through an experience designed by you.

10 – Time on site / page views. These are related to bounce rate in that the longer a visitor spends looking at your content the more Google understands that it's high quality and the more likely they are to promote your site in the search results. To optimize this you'll need to consistently add pages, posts and content to your site.

Ideally, you'd monitor your site weekly and optimize new content as you create it. It's unrealistic to think you can do all this along with all that your design business requires of you. Understanding the basic principles of SEO as you build out your site will help you create a site that's better than most other architects and designers.

I always focus more on creating helpful, useful, and shareable content than I do on writing for the search engines. If Google is doing their job properly, then building valuable content is an evergreen strategy because Google's mission is to filter the best content of the web and deliver it to users searching for that information.

Tools and Resources

Beginners Guide to SEO (by Moz.com): this free, in-depth guide will tell you more than you ever wanted to know about SEO in an accessible format.

MozBar: a real-time browser plug-in to highlight areas of your site that need SEO work.

WordPress SEO: plug-in for WordPress by Yoast. Short-cut to optimizing your website's content.

Google Analytics: shows how people use and interact with your website. It's an essential tool for monitoring bounce rates, visitor count, page loads, and other problems.

Google Webmaster Tools: diagnostic tools for assessing and optimizing your page to be Google-friendly. Connect this with your analytics.

Bing Webmaster Tools: similar to the above but owned by Microsoft.

MailChimp: free e-mail service provider (up to 2,000 subscribers). Autoresponder is paid.

AWeber: 30-day trial offer for $1, $19/month thereafter.

SumoMe: one of many available e-mail list builder plug-ins for WordPress. Create pop-ups and redirects to build your e-mail list.

LeadPages: squeeze page plug-in for WordPress.

OptinForms: e-mail sign-up box plug-in for WordPress.

Website statistics tracking: Many options available, check the iTunes or Android store. I use the Analytiks iPhone app because it's simple and it looks good.

Keyword Suggestion Tool: Google Keyword Planner or type in a phrase over at Über suggest and it delivers an alphabetically sorted list of terms you can use to target.

6 | Getting Hired

"Everybody is a genius. But if you judge a fish by its ability to climb a tree, it will live its whole life believing that it is stupid." - Albert Einstein

Now that you've structured your business, crafted a brand and you've started marketing your message, you'll begin to receive inquiries from potential clients for your products and services. In marketing parlance, these potential clients are called leads. At this point your job is to convert those leads into paying clients and their projects into billable work, which can be difficult even for a seasoned professional. For you, the new firm owner, it's a monumental task.

You've honed your design chops in school and under the tutelage of established firms; you're more than capable of getting the work done. However, to a prospective client that's not all that matters. It's not your design skills that will get you hired. People expect good design and there are many skilled designers in the world.

Clients are looking for someone capable of solving *their* particular problem. They're looking for someone they can get along with, someone who listens, and someone they can trust to manage their project. Don't make the mistake of thinking it's all about you; it's not about your design skills or your aesthetic. Design usually ranks quite low on the list of priorities for your client. Budget is usually higher, unless you're fortunate enough to work with clients for whom budget is irrelevant. Knowing this, you can tailor your pitch toward solving your client's problems rather than making it about your design prowess. This will help to distinguish you from your competition.

Part of the reason design is prioritized so low is that many clients are unfamiliar with the design process; it's a black box of sorts. For them to invest a large sum of money into that black box you'll need a system for earning their respect and winning their trust. Your job is to educate them, about what you do, about how you can help them and to make them feel at ease.

Qualifying Leads. When someone contacts you, by e-mail, a phone call or drops in to your office, congratulations are due. This truly is a marketing win. Recognize that you've already sold the potential client on many things. After all, they felt confident enough in your abilities to reach out and take the next step with you.

From here, you'll need to qualify the lead to determine whether they'll be a good fit for your business and the kind of work you do (or want to do). Of the many ways to qualify leads, perhaps the most common is an initial phone call followed by a face-to-face meeting, either at the project site, in the client's home or in your office. But, there are new ways, which can also be effective. Marketing funnels that vet a client before you even speak with them. But let's start with the most traditional first.

Phone Interview. Set up a time to discuss the potential project and develop a list of questions that will help qualify them. Use the phone interview to gauge the lead's commitment to the principles that guide your business. Talk about fees early, you don't want to waste too much time with someone looking for a service that doesn't correlate to what you're offering.

The phone interview is about triage. If they balk at your general pricing guidelines, send them to a product you've developed that more closely aligns with the level of service they're seeking. Use it as an opportunity to generate passive income and capitalize on a lead most would let walk away. Think about digital products, guides, courses, plan sets, handbooks, and checklists that would provide some of the value you offer at a much lower cost.

Qualifying questions reveal a client's personality traits and provide a wealth of information. You'll see patterns and clues in the answers that will aid you as you evaluate whether to take on a project or to meet with them at all. Take notes and think equally about what a client reveals or chooses not to reveal during your exchange.

Some potential questions you may consider asking:

Tell me more about your project, what are the project goals? This question forces the lead to articulate the scope of work in real terms. The priorities should be obvious in their response. A recent potential lead of mine wrote a long meandering description and ended by saying, "We don't really know what we want." Red flag. I met with them, because a few of their ideas sounded interesting, but the meeting bore the fruit of their initial e-mail – they were indecisive and unsure of what they wanted.

What is your time frame? This determines whether the project will fit in your schedule and it also gauges how serious they are. Vague timelines suggest they're casual shoppers and not ready to commit. I generally avoid these interviews.

There will be clients ready to begin construction in, "a month or so." Again, this usually signals a client with unreasonable expectations that will be hard to please. It's easy to respond by saying, "the earliest I could begin working on your project would be, _____. From there I would expect a timeline of X months for design." Don't make your occupation trying to please difficult clients, prescreening is meant to flag them for you to avoid.

Are you speaking with other architects / designers? You need to understand the competitive landscape to best position yourself. If they say they're speaking with more than three designers, I'll always refuse the interview (unless I need the practice). This kind of behavior speaks of indecision, and you have little chance of getting the job. Sometimes refusing the interview will actually spur on their interest. Creating scarcity in the market is always a good thing.

If they answer yes, and it's a few, I follow up with: **Who else are you speaking with?** If they list other local firms of similar quality to you, that's helpful information and a good sign that their expectations and assumptions about you are accurate.

What is the budget you've allocated to the project? An unreasonable budget can be corrected through education and by tweaking the size and program of the project, within reason. Although an unrealistic budget isn't grounds for immediate dismissal, you should proceed with caution.

The budget question will tell you whether you're best positioned to serve this client. For example, I know that I'm not the most cost-efficient choice for clients with projects below $400,000. The reason? I'm expensive. My fees on smaller projects constitute a larger portion of the overall budget and I'm open about this fact at the before we even begin and design work. Don't try to be everyone's solution, there will be clients you're just not a good fit for; be honest from the outset.

Follow-up with, **What if the work costs more than you want to spend?** Because it usually does. Their answer will be an indicator of how they deal with the unpleasant and their tolerance for financial uncertainty. It may also confirm that "the budget" isn't really "the budget," and that there's some extra padding that they've saved.

Do you have any particular stylistic preferences? Most architects and designers pride themselves on being stylistically neutral. But, like it or not, we all have a certain working style. Because I practice in an architecturally historically rich part of the world, I've worked in offices that accepted work that was stylistically divergent from the work they did best or actually wanted to do. They accepted the work because they needed to fill billable time slots. When completed, these projects never bolstered their portfolios, only their bank accounts. I ask this question because there are only a limited number of projects I'll have time to complete in my life. I'm not interested in doing work I'm not best suited for – it's not fair to me or my client.

Have you worked with other architects or designers before? This is an important question. If yes and they've used another local option, there's probably a reason they're not moving ahead with them. You need to know more. If no, you have some educating to do; you'll need to carefully explain all the costs involved and your process. Be as detailed as you can.

Follow up a yes with: **How did it work out?** A difficult or hard to please client will often reveal their true self in their follow-up response. You want to learn whether the previous designer's process was different from yours and whether it was a collaborative relationship or a confrontational one.

Why do you need a designer? Their answer will tell you how you'll be valued in the process. Some clients will say, "I just need a drawing or two" or "I have a floor plan in mind" or "I have all the materials picked out I just need help ordering." These are all red flags that they don't understand or value what a designer or architect can add to the process. If someone is looking for me to revamp or tweak a purchased floor plan, I refuse the job. It's a liability and potential copyright concern to avoid.

Who will be making the decisions? And how do you arrive at decisions? If there's a follow-up meeting, you want to be sure the person making the decisions will be present. It's valuable to understand how they view the decision-making process and how capable they are of coming to an agreement on divergent solutions. You don't want to be the instrument of one party or another in a long-standing argument of design aesthetics or taste between spouses.

How did you hear about me? You want clients who want to work with you because of the work you do, not because you're a drafting service or a warm (local) body with professional experience. Equally, this is a self-serving question because it can guide and hone your marketing efforts. Knowing how someone found you and what kind of lead that person turned out to be (good or bad) is valuable information.

OPTIONAL:

Tell me a little about yourself and what do you do for a living? You may or may not be comfortable asking this in your first meeting. I look for ways to weave it into natural conversation, and some will tell you without you having to ask. Even though this is a form of profiling, the way someone is compensated sets the tone for how the project will move ahead and can make difficult budget discussions (usually) much more reasonable.

Please rate the following priorities for your project. function, aesthetic, design, quality, budget, and schedule. This one is best done via e-mail; it forces a discussion of what's most and least important. It may also reveal conflicts – budget and schedule are common ones.

Automated Prequalification. This alternative to the traditional phone interview can automate the prequalification process for you. The idea with an automated system is to establish a sign-up process that covers all the questions you and a potential client have before you ever meet. All the prequalifying steps can be built into the automated funnel without having to spend time on them.

We can use the same e-mail list management pipeline discussed in Chapter 5 to automate the process. The lead magnet here is directed at a potential client looking to work with you. It should clearly illustrate what you do best and the kind of work you're seeking.

Are you focusing on renovation work? Then develop a guide that talks about the 8 mistakes people most often make when renovating. Targeting bathroom remodels? Create a handbook listing the highest resale or value-adds in the bathroom. New construction? Ten hidden costs you need to be aware of in new construction. The idea with all of these is twofold, first to collect their e-mail address and secondly to position you as the expert.

In MailChimp (or AWeber) you'll want to create a new list called, "New Client Funnel." On the Contact page of your website you want to clearly state your call-to-action for the potential lead. It might say, "Schedule Your Consultation," or "Ready to begin your project?" Create a large colored button on this page and embed the URL for the sign-up in the button along with the call-to-action text. The text on the contact page should describe the process you're about to walk them through and the lead magnet on offer. Once a lead signs up they will be directed through your automated prequalification process.

Instead of drafting the typical "Thank you for signing up" e-mail in the double opt-in, substitute your prequalification e-mail. Begin by thanking them for their interest and describe your process briefly. Don't make it too long. If there's more explaining to do link out to other pages (FAQ, etc.) on your website so they can find more information if they need it. The primary purpose of this e-mail is to ask the prequalifying questions you would normally ask in a phone interview.

Replies can be filtered by you or a virtual assistant and triaged based on your criteria (schedule, budget, project type, etc.) Qualified leads, the ones you're interested in, can be followed up with directly and will proceed to the next step in your sales process. That may be a free or paid consultation, or a new client welcome package. Either way, you'll probably want to schedule an in-person meeting next.

The automated series could keep working for you with your qualified leads by sending out a list of the documents they'll need to gather and complete to begin the design process (see Chapter 11 for more on SOPs). Attach your new client welcome package, service list, client survey, contract, existing conditions requirements, survey requirements, etc.

If they're not a good fit the follow-up should thank them for their interest, describe the reason you're not the right designer for them, refer them to alternative resources (developed for sale by you) and perhaps offer a referral to another pro in your area that may better serve their needs. As always, be courteous and helpful, you're still marketing even when you're saying no.

The point of automation is to keep you from having to go through a series of repetitive tasks each week. The exact process described may not be right for your business, but take inspiration from the idea of automation not the specific execution.

Another way to think about it is to think about how you can educate this potential lead. Indoctrinate them on your particular process. Walk them through it one e-mail or video at a time. While you're teaching them about what you do, you'll be making them comfortable with an unknown and complicated process and simultaneously prove that you're best positioned to help them.

The key here is that it's *your* process.

This approach is a soft sell on your services and the value you add. You can talk about your fees, what the typical steps you'll be taking together are, things to watch out for, and the value of approaching a project the way you do. This exchange takes the place of the questions that invariably consume the first thirty minutes (or more) of the interview. Questions like: How do you work? What are your fees? What's the process for making changes? How will I visualize the design? Who makes up the design team?

Preemptively answer these questions once. This way, the time you spend together at the initial meeting can be used to discuss the details of their specific project and what you can do to help rather than answer the same questions repeatedly.

It's an altogether more efficient process and a better use of everyone's time.

Think of the list of questions a potential client may have about what you do and try to answer them before you ever meet. Set these e-mails to be delivered on a timeline of your choosing using your e-mail marketing program after a potential client first contacts you. This, I guarantee, will distinguish you from your competition.

The end result will be a lead that's been prequalified and someone already predisposed to your method of working. You've educated them on the process – your process – and if they're interested they'll take the next step with you because they like what they've heard, understand the value you offer and perhaps most importantly, the costs involved.

Prequalifying Process. Regardless of whether or not you decide to automate the prequalifying process the idea with all these questions is to vet a client enough to decide whether or not to meet for the first time together. Even though initial meetings are an hour or less, that's time many professionals don't bill for – lost revenue. If you find that after the first meeting you're saying no to too many clients, you might revisit your qualifying questions to better filter your prospects.

Before the Interview. When your business is new you need a means of standing out and the best way I've found is to over-deliver. Give people far more than they've asked for, surprise them. Make this your brand's promise. You don't have to wait until the first meeting to begin over-delivering. Each of the following is a means of over-delivering and it's a first chance for you to convey your attention to detail and your thoroughness.

> **'What to Expect' Document.** This is a branded process document that describes in detail the steps you'll be taking together. Never underestimate the amount of handholding people need throughout the design process. Sending this document also offers the chance to restate your interest in their project and to confirm the meeting date and time. I e-mail it, but you may prefer to print it and send it by snail mail.
>
> **Communication.** Courteous, thoughtful and prompt responses to any correspondence will set the tone for your relationship. Many established pros don't get this right. Because you're not quite as busy (and swamped with

phone calls and e-mails) as they are, good communication is a business fundamental where you can easily outmaneuver your competition.

I also pay careful attention to the responses I receive (or don't receive) from a potential client. This will be more important in the future if you're offered the job, after the interview.

Research. Step into your potential client's shoes for a moment and do your best to understand their particular problem. I like to spend a little time studying the general project constraints (neighborhood, zoning, codes, etc.) before the interview. I gather this information and keep it in an Evernote folder for the project to review right before the interview. A small amount of background research proves to a client that you're genuinely interested and invested in their project from the very first meeting and it makes it more likely that you'll be remembered after the interview. I also note whether or not this client fits my ideal client avatar. If it doesn't, my marketing needs adjusting.

Personalized Service. Connect with the person behind the project. People decide who they're going to work with based on many things, but high on that list is emotional connection. People hire other people. You can dispel the myth of the aloof design professional by being genuine and interested in the people you'll be designing for. Good design relies on your ability to understand who they are and what's important to them. It's also simply part of being a good human in the world.

Standard Operating Procedures (SOPs)
When a prospective client – a new lead – contacts your business you'll need a procedure for handling them. This standard operating procedure (SOP) will consistently welcome and engage these prospects into your business and ensure you don't have to expend energy thinking about what to do when someone contacts you other than implementing the SOP. Much like your marketing plan, this SOP will be a working document that you'll refine with time.

The SOP documents can be developed for any phase of work and Chapter 11 describes them in both general and detailed terms. For on-boarding clients you'll want to prequalify, gather specific information about the project, and develop a fee proposal. I like to walk through each step in my process and make sure there's a correlating document I can assign to it.

Action Items: Develop your prequalification question list or an automated process. Draft your branded new client package of information and your SOPs. Be sure to include at least the following:

> New client package (welcome letter, process description or guidebook, fee chart, description of expectations, possibly a contract sample, etc.)
>
> Client contact information
>
> Physical location and directions
>
> Project brief and any initial notes
>
> Estimated budget
>
> Code and regulation compliance checklist
>
> References and testimonials (I don't send these initially, but I have them on-hand)
>
> Marketing triage (How did this client find you? Use to fine-tune your marketing efforts.)

The Interview

Most leads will want to meet with you in person after having reviewed your business online, read your 'About' page, and confirmed that you're capable of doing the kind of work they're seeking. The interview is your chance to personally introduce your brand and to connect with the lead. I try to resist repeating what I've said on my website because at this stage clients are looking to make a deeper connection with you. They're looking for reasons to hire you over another designer.

I look at the interview as a chance to accomplish three things:

> **1 – Information gathering.** Both you and the potential client are trying to decide whether or not this will be a good fit. Listen to the way the client states the problem and restate it back to him or her. You don't have to provide solutions yet; you have to show that you're capable of being a good listener.

Your success as a designer relies on how well you're able to listen to a problem, articulate it and then provide a solution. Listening ensures that a client will feel engaged, important, and relevant to the process. Equally you want to understand how a client thinks and values design.

You should be asking questions of the client and taking notes (budget, schedule, goals, style, etc.) If you view it as a conversation rather than a one-sided interview you'll be more relaxed and genuine. I resist any attempt to make the first meeting about providing design advice or solutions in the interview by referring to the design process documents, which lay out an iterative process through which the design reveals itself.

2 – Describe the design process. If you've set up an automated prequalification process skip this section. Even though you've sent this document to the lead right after they set up the interview, you should walk them through your process. Pull back the curtain on what you actually do by showing them a real project. I find that people really enjoy looking behind the scenes at how a project is taken from conceptual idea to reality. It's also a good way to showcase your portfolio without merely doing a walk-through (this is the kitchen, this is the mudroom). I like to describe my process as a narrative that's told through the images in my portfolio, which are centered about the story of my clients. Don't make it about the architecture make it about the client. This sets people at ease because you're talking about people not abstract design concepts.

3 – Chemistry. The final thing the interview does is to gauge whether or not there's any chemistry between you. It's intangible and hard to quantify, but you have a lifetime of experience to guide you in understanding personal chemistry. You'll be entering into a long-term and deeply personal relationship; it should be with someone you can connect with and respect.

I don't like the idea of trying to sell myself too hard in an interview. Even if you have no projects on your boards at the time of the interview you want to appear in-demand, with plenty of work and of course, confident. In no way do you want to appear desperate for a client's job.

This isn't to say that your first few interviews won't be really intimidating. But with each subsequent interview it will get easier. Certain questions will be asked over and over again.

The boilerplate questions people ask usually come from the American Institute of Architects online guide for clients among others. Given a modicum of experience you won't even need to think about the answers to most of these common questions. Early on just make sure you've read and prepared answers for each of the most commons ones.

There's always a new question that surprises me now and again. So what happens then -- what if they ask a question you can't answer? Honesty is always the best policy. Don't bluff your way through it. "I don't know the answer, but I'll gladly look into it and get back to you," is far better than undermining your credibility by delivering false information.

Be prepared to pivot their questions and reframe them in a way that you think is more important. My fees are higher than my competitors so I have to be able to justify that when asked. My answer? Even though my fee is 5-10% higher than my competitor's my finished homes typically appraise at 20-25% above comparable homes. That's an immediate return on your investment of 10-20% and that's before you take into account the added value an architect's design brings to the utility, efficiency, quality and improved aesthetics of a home. Rephrase objections about cost into value added.

If you build the automated marketing funnel discussed above, you can head off many of these questions before the initial interview. This will save both of you some time and anxiety and get right into the business of talking about the project rather than answering rote questions again and again. The automated process brings you much closer to closing the sale.

I find that building in scarcity into my services actually creates demand. I tell every client that I choose my projects based on their merits and best fit not on schedule, project type or budget. This is a position of power and it's a great spot to bargain from. Arrive at the interview knowing that you don't need this job. The idea that you'll accept this job only if it's the right fit for your business is a much better way to reframe the interview. You'll come across as more self-assured and you'll project an air of professionalism that will hopefully be irresistible.

Ideally you want to be in the position of selecting the jobs you take on not the job selecting you. Of course that isn't always a reality; there will be projects you have to take for the strategic relationship it forges or for the money.

As a rule, I'll never take a job where I have a bad feeling about the client in our initial interactions, even if my workload is thinner than I'd like. I recognize that our relationship is a long one and it will be tested often by very stressful financial and emotional situations. Working through the design process with a difficult or unfriendly client isn't enjoyable in any way. It's no way to earn a living and the projects that result from those collaborations aren't usually something you'll want to promote.

It's your business you get to make the choice. Isn't that an empowering thought?

Focus on the Client. Try to make the meeting about the client and their particular project or problem rather than you. Make sure they understand how you're best positioned to solve that problem via your process. Understand that people will be buying a solution to their problem not a designer's ego.

Clients are self-centered. They care a lot about how you'll approach solving their problem and a lot less about your accomplishments and theory of design. The interview is an opportunity to show that you know more about their project than the others they'll be speaking with. Take the time to print out a plan of their neighborhood or a Google Earth view and use it to talk about their specific location, what's unique about it or a little known restriction affecting the area.

A client will remember that you were the one who took the initiative to research and understand the problem and that makes a difference when they're deciding who the best person is for the job.

A Conversation. Keeping the interview in a conversational tone will relax everyone. Remember that you're interviewing them too. Don't think of the interview as a live demonstration where you must prove your design skill set as you walk through a space or pore over a floor plan. Rather, think of it as a discussion about finding the best solution to the client's problem.

This is a sizeable investment for you and your potential client. You'll be investing your business resources and crafting your brand, make sure it marries with your mission and aesthetic sensibilities. If it doesn't you're not serving the client's needs or your own. Don't accept the work.

94

Personalities. Typically people are on their best behavior during an initial meeting. This means that any personality conflicts you notice during the interview will only be amplified during the design and construction process. You'll build the skills necessary to discern the subtle 'tells' a client offers during an interview over time. My advice is to trust your instincts and learn to read the things people convey with their body language; it will serve you well.

Charging for the First Meeting. I think it's hard for a new business (and even an established business) to charge for an initial consultation. The first meeting is really an opportunity for both you and the client to interview each other.

Knowing this should actually relieve some of the pressure you feel. You want to know more about them and gauge whether this will be a good fit for you too. Design is a commitment of many months, sometimes years, of your business' resources; the interview is the first step towards making sure it's a good fit for <u>both</u> of you.

When you're just getting started, I believe that practicing your interviewing skills on a real human is more valuable to you than any financial gain to be had from an initial meeting. By offering a free consultation you'll speak with more clients than if you charge for one. But you'll also speak with less serious clients – the shoppers.

Use each interview as a chance to hone your presentation and sales pitch, you'll hear a broad range of questions and you'll invariably make mistakes. That's worth more than anything else to you as you build your business.

As you gain more work or decide that the cost of doing all of these interviews and the time they consume is too much, you can move on to charge for the visit. The benefit of charging is that it immediately defines you as the professional in your relationship and ties the discussions to a value exchange. Potential clients are usually unfamiliar with the process and have expectations of a first meeting that are just plain unrealistic. I had a prospect request on an initial interview that "we" begin sketching out ideas together, right then and there, before I was even hired (or accepted the job)!

Charging for your interview time - typically one to two hours - means you'll be paid to offer the valuable advice you previously gave for free. It also means that you don't have to hold back. The paid interview will also limit the number of leads you'll be talking with and you'll be assured that they're serious. You might consider crediting them the fee if they hire you. This offers a reward to a client for hiring you to do the project while you get the reward of having the job. Meanwhile any errant shoppers will still compensate you for your time.

If you employ an automated prequalification process you may find that charging for the first consultation is a natural progression, the final step in your series of e-mails. The final e-mail can link to a page on your website which talks about the next steps. The next step logical step would be to book an in-person consultation with you. Naturally, this costs money, right? You don't book a consultation with a doctor or a lawyer and expect it to be free do you? You're controlling the process to manage expectations and educate the potential client on the way things work in the design industry.

There's a common marketing technique called price anchoring that I like to use. Price anchoring works like this: for any product or service there are essentially three pricing tiers. You've seen this used everywhere, especially in fast food restaurants, because it works. The lowest price tier obviously has the least number of features, it's the stripped down model. The middle tier adds some key features to the basic feature set, a good all-around choice. The highest price product has everything you'd ever want, all the bells and whistles.

The middle price anchors the other two. It not only gives the other two a reason for being, it validates the overall price range. People aren't aware of the costs involved when it comes to custom design. Price anchoring describes it plainly. The middle anchor will appeal to most people because they will assume they don't need all of the added features of the highest price tier and the lowest price tier is likely to be missing something they actually want. Equally, people don't often want to appear cheap. One of the advantages of anchoring is that when viewed in this manner people intuitively understand that your time has value.

How can you put it to work in your business?

Begin by defining the services you'll offer and set your price anchor. The middle price is what most people will choose; let's assume this is your one-hour consultation in their home. For this you set a price equal to two times your hourly rate – let's say $300. I say two times because you want the lowest price tier to be the least amount of time you're willing to invest in qualifying a lead. Anything less than one-hour of time is difficult to bill for so let's say that's one-hour a hypothetical $150. The highest tier may be two and a half times the middle tier, $750 in this example.

The lowest tier might be for a phone consultation with no deliverables. The middle tier is the in-home consultation with a written project brief and fee estimate as the deliverable. The top tier is the middle tier plus a detailed breakdown of the project brief, a budget estimate, and one possible solution. This is just an example; your deliverables will likely be different.

On your website, you can add a "Book Your Consultation Package Now" button linked to PayPal. When the lead books the package they'll prepay for it, which will trigger an e-mail to you and you'll schedule the consultation.

Because client's can have some unrealistic visions of what actually happens in an initial interview (as in the previous example) it's your job to set the tone and lead the discussion. It offers you the chance to show that you're a professional who can guide them through an unfamiliar and complicated process.

Action Items: Develop an interview SOP. Include a standard format for the interview, a list of questions for your potential client and an anticipated list of the possible questions your client may ask you. At the end of the document include a standard list of documents to have on hand prior to each interview (site plan, Google Earth view, etc.).

Experience and Ignorance

As I close out this chapter I wanted to offer some inspiration to you on the journey through your first set of interviews and on to getting hired. This can be one of the most disheartening times in a new business owner's evolution. You'll face constant reminders that your business is a fledgling. You have less experience in the market. I've been at this for almost 20 years and it's still an issue.

The found of TED, Richard Saul Wurman, produced a wonderful documentary on the story of Charles and Ray Eames called, "Eames: The Architect and the Painter." In it Wurman says the following, referring to Charles: "Sell your expertise and you have a limited repertoire. Sell your ignorance and you have an unlimited repertoire. He was selling his ignorance and his desire to learn about a subject. The journey of not knowing to knowing was his work."

Let this guide you as you build your business from a place of relative inexperience. The Eames used their inexperience as a methodology for discovering ingenious design solutions. Their narrative actually capitalized and profited from their ignorance on a particular subject. As such they could reframe problems and seek novel solutions.

As a new business owner try to get comfortable selling your inexperience and your ignorance. You can offer clients a fresh approach to their problem and bring an exuberance and willingness to learn that seasoned pros gave up long ago. Clients understand that new businesses will often work harder to achieve outstanding results as they're building their reputations.

Not every client will appreciate this and that's okay. You'll have to accept that some clients won't hire you because your business is new and lacks a proven track record. Hearing for the first time from a prospective client, "I'm sorry but we've chosen to go with a firm that has more experience," isn't easy. I can tell you from experience, it's demoralizing. The first time I heard it I thought about all of the years of professional education, my years of internship, the professional licensing process, and years designing, drawing, detailing, project management and field experience. How much more experience was this client looking for?

What I've come to understand is that there are two possible reasons for a response like that. First, that was a client who was looking for a sure thing. In design and construction, that just doesn't exist. I can't personally guarantee the success of a project, I can do my best to guide it and offer my professional advice, but no amount of experience makes an architectural project a sure bet.

The second thing I learned, and the more valuable lesson, is that I actually didn't convey my experience level well enough. I wasn't confident or convincing to them in the face of my direct competition. The architect they hired to do the work was a professional of similar age and experience level and he was better able to convey that to the client. Lesson learned.

The first reason is a predisposition of a particular client. The second is something I could learn from and work on. This is why I recommend practicing your interviewing skills at every possible chance you get. Practicing on real clients forces you to be more spontaneous and field a variety of questions in a way that won't sound scripted. It will also hone your listening skills.

Clients want to leave the interview with two primary things. First, to feel confident that you're a professional with the skills to complete their project and second, that they've made an emotional connection with you, they're comfortable around you and that you care about their project. If you satisfy these basic needs there's a much higher likelihood of you getting the job - assuming you want it.

Most of all be you. Dispense with the lofty designer attitude and linguistics. Use conversation and narrative rather than lecturing to talk openly about what you do and convey your excitement for your profession. Genuine passion is contagious. Even if you don't secure the commission you'll have educated someone in the world about what architects and designers do for a living and your presentation next time will be that much better.

There are clients out there that will take a risk on your inexperienced business and hire you in spite of it. If you determine it's a good fit, this one client and project can be all the spring-board you'll need to build your referral network and establish an unending supply of new work of your choosing.

Getting Hired
After the interview is over you'll want to follow-up with the client. Develop one e-mail and save it as a template to use as

the starting point for you correspondence (be sure to add this to your SOP). This way you're not reinventing it each time, but you'll still have room to personalize it and tailor it to each specific client.

If you've promised to follow-up on anything (fee proposal, references, etc.) tell the client when they can expect it from you. If there are any unanswered questions you had be sure to request answers to those as well.

I add my initial impressions, concerns and project specific information to the meeting notes I take immediately following the interview while it's still fresh in my mind. I take a photo of this and file it in the corresponding 'prospective client' folder I maintain within Evernote. I also add any site photos if the meeting was held on-site.

Declining the Job (or saying "No, thanks.")

One of your most important jobs as CEO is learning when to say no. After the interview you should have a fairly good sense for whether or not you'd accept the job if offered. When you're just getting things up and running it's easy to fall into the trap of accepting anything and everything that comes along, especially when you're staring at empty boards and no revenue.

Revenue aside, you want to invest your time and business resources into projects that will become the foundation of your brand. The early projects are especially crucial in this regard.

Here's a list of things to look out for and guide your decision to accept a project or let it pass you by:

> **Misaligned budgets.** Refusing to accept average costs of design or construction in your area is a red flag for a client with unreasonable expectations.
>
> **Very small budgets.** These can consume massive amounts of time and are often wed to picky clients.
>
> **Expectations.** We can't expect non-professionals to have a sense for all of the costs involved in construction, but if we offer professional advice and it's readily dismissed it's a warning sign that the client may have unrealistic expectations. Someone unwilling to accept your professional advice is a bad partner.

Communication Issues. If a client doesn't respond to you in a timely manner you can bet that those patterns will extend to paying bills and other aspects of your professional relationship. Early patterns will be amplified under the stressful conditions of mounting design fees and escalating construction costs.

Is the project a good fit? Does the client's vision align with yours? There's no sense in designing a historical renovation if you're pursuing modern, minimalist cottage designs. Make sure your brand mission will be represented in the final product. It's a disservice to you and your client to do otherwise.

Is the person a good fit? Can you imagine spending time with this person? The project and client go hand in hand. You may love the project but find the client difficult. The two are inseparable; it takes both to make it a successful endeavor. Trust your gut; your first impression of someone is rarely wrong.

Ask around in your network about your prospect; do they have a good reputation or a bad one? During a recent interview I had a few inklings that a particular client may be difficult so I started asking around. A builder friend of mine was working on a lot adjacent to this particular client. The builder quickly confirmed my reservations and the client's true nature were quickly revealed through a few choice interactions. The project was attractive but the client wasn't right.

Try to think as dispassionately as possible, this is a business decision not an emotional one. You may really like the client, but if the project isn't right it's a poor match.

Saying no to a client who is ready to hire you can feel like a difficult task but once you prepare the SOP and an e-mail template response you'll never have to think about it again. Just recall the template, personalize it a little and send it.

I prefer, "I'm not the right architect for your project," to almost anything else. There's also, "This isn't a good fit between my strengths and your needs." It recognizes their project as viable and emphasizes that you're acting in the best interest of the project not you. It seems outwardly less selfish.

There are other ways to decline a project too. If the schedule is too aggressive politely saying, "I'm not able serve the project schedule given my current project load," is an easy out. If you can make a client understand that you're interested in meeting their needs not yours they'll understand. If they don't, and this has happened to me on more than one occasion, you'll have seen a side of them that will reinforce your decision to refuse the work.

Trying to out-price a difficult client is a bad idea. Consider what you'll do if the client accepts. They'll understand it's a high fee and be willing to squeeze out every last cent from their expenditure and from you. Difficult clients are accustomed to exorbitant fees and often have the budgets to support their bad behavior. This is a bad way to say no.

Waiting lists can be a great tool for maintaining a supply of good projects waiting in the wings until you have the time to work on them. But don't use them as a queue for second rate projects or ill-fitting clients.

No = Yes. Remember that every no is also a yes to something else. Your business and your brand has a set of priorities, saying no to a bad project only reinforces them. It leaves the door open for the work and clients that are a better fit.

It's hard to walk away from a perfectly viable project. Rather than thinking of turning work away as lost revenue think of it as an investment in freedom. The freedom to choose the best clients and projects is a good thing for everyone involved – you, your client, and your business. Your brand demands this of you, be a good steward.

The Offer (or not). If you've left the interview thinking you'd accept the commission if offered, that's excellent news. Hopefully the potential client came away with a similar feeling.

Waiting for a response from design clients isn't easy. During the interview I always ask about the timeline for selecting a designer, even if I've already asked during prequalification. It's an easy ask because it pairs well with the conversation about construction schedule.

Follow up with prospective clients as often as you feel comfortable but you'll have to strike a balance between seeming desperate and professionally interested. Too many follow-ups and you'll appear desperate; too few and you risk them forgetting about you.

What works for me: I have an e-mail template that I customize and send out after the interview - usually on the same day. The following day I send a hard copy of my welcome package (see the next section) to the prospect via snail mail. I then wait until about a week after their "decision date" has elapsed and follow-up with an e-mail.

Here's the trick, this e-mail isn't selling anything at all. I copy a link to a project on ArchDaily.com (or another appropriate site) that's similar to their project saying, "I saw this today and thought of you. Hope this finds you well." If I really want the project, I'll purchase a book on Amazon and send it directly to them with a short message. This works really well.

These tactics are designed to remind them of their project. People will often delay making important decisions like hiring a designer because it's a big commitment – financially and emotionally. Building and renovation projects typically incubate in a client's mind for a long time before they act on them. Your goal is to get them to act by reminding them that you're ready to help them take the initial steps toward completing it.

The first e-mail is sent out of courtesy – a "thank you for selecting me out of the many choices you had" kind of e-mail. The physical welcome package arrives in their mailbox a few days later and provides them with tangible evidence of the fruits of the meeting. People love getting snail mail; it's universal. That package lets them know that you do what you say you're going to in a timely manner and it's a chance to highlight your design skills too (nice graphics, well-worded). The third point of contact shows you're still interested and that you listened to what they said in the interview by showing them a similar project to theirs. It also reminds them that you're a designer with the skills to curate their ideas into physical reality. It shows them that you think in visual terms.

If you're offered the job, congratulations! Your marketing and sales process has proven itself effective. Now you'll move on to new challenges and deliver the work you promised. If you're not offered the job don't be discouraged. There's always a next project, don't take it as a personal affront on your talents. If at all possible solicit the client's reasoning behind their decision. You don't have anything to lose, the worst they can do is to not reply and if they do reply you'll be armed with more information to make your sales pitch better next time. Tweak your SOP accordingly.

You'll quickly come to realize that there will be more jobs that you don't get than ones that you do – this is especially true if you're a sole practitioner. It's simply a matter of scale. But knowing this doesn't make the early interviews any less ego-bruising. Persevere and push through, your break will come.

The Welcome Package

Once you've been hired, you should have some sort of a welcome packet of materials developed.

Include:
- Welcome letter
- Contract
- Business card
- Step-by-step process outline
- New client questionnaire
- List of services and rates
- FAQ (if you have one)

This sets a professional tone for your relationship and builds confidence early that you're attending to all of the details. Depending on the demographic you're targeting, the welcome package doesn't have to be a physical document or package. In fact, if possible try to make it a secure online page with links to each of the documents above. Set up a template e-mail with the link to this page that you can direct your new client to and the on-boarding process will be streamlined. A web-based solution allows you to easily update it with new information (rates, schedules, questions, contracts) without wasting paper or ink and saves you the postage costs and hassle of mailing out physical documents.

7 | Getting Paid

(Your Contract)

"Ever tried. Ever failed. No matter. Try again. Fail again. Fail better." – Samuel Beckett

So you've moved a prospective lead through your sales process and converted them into a client ready to hire you. You're ready to begin designing, you can handle the tasks of project delivery – programming, design, and drawing – but there are a few key steps that you probably weren't involved in as an employee working for someone else. First, you need a framework that describes the terms of your relationship and a binding agreement on the terms of compensation and that means signing a contract.

Contract
I'll begin by reiterating the fact that I'm an architect, not a lawyer. Please don't construe my advice as having legal authority of any kind. The gravitas of contractual decisions as it relates to your personal and business futures deserves review by a lawyer. This is actually one area where the AIA (American Institute of Architects) proves its value. If you're a member, they can help with legal advice, but more on this later.

Getting your contract signed, in many states, is a legal precursor to beginning design work. Even if it isn't a requirement in your state, a contract protects you and your client and it's necessary to formalize the terms of your relationship. It's also a meticulous written reminder of all the complexity pregnant in the design and construction process. There's a lot that can go wrong along the way and the contract describes the legal contingencies for handling those possibilities.

You've never written a contract, where do you begin?

If you're still working for someone else, and assuming you're pursuing similar work for your new business, find and read through the contract for the project you're currently working on. Study it thoroughly and take note of the specifics that an actual client in your jurisdiction has agreed to. Use this as supporting documentation and reference material, but it's not yours and it's likely that your firm paid a lawyer to customize to their needs so don't copy it.

Perhaps the easiest place though to begin is by visiting the AIA's website. The AIA has a reputation throughout the design trades as having the gold standard in contracts. This is because their contracts have a history of being tested in the courts and refined over decades. They persist because they have a strong legal track record. Although they're generally perceived as fair contracts, they do have a reputation in construction law for being especially friendly to the design professional. Good for you certainly, but if your client has a lawyer you can expect some wording may be up for discussion if you use their contract as your agreement.

The AIA offers contracts tailored to every scale of project and relationship between parties you can conjure. The B-series documents are the ones you're interested in at this stage. These are the Owner (or Developer) / Architect agreements. Peruse the various options on their site to determine the best fit for the scale of project that you'll be undertaking.

As a first step, before buying anything, I recommend you trade your e-mail address for their Small Project Contract Guide (free), which will help you determine which contract is right for you. While you're there read a few of the small project documents, see what they cover and note the wording that's used; it will give you a better idea of what your contract should include.

The basic sections you'll need in your contract are:

> Parties of the Agreement: Architect, Owner/Developer/Federal Gov't...
> Project Description
> Architect's Responsibilities (including scope of services)
> Owner's Responsibilities
> Compensation Terms
> Termination
> Copyright Notice regarding the drawings and digital files.

You want to be certain that the document clearly describes what's included (Basic Services) and what isn't included (Additional Services) in your fee. I have a menu of additional services that's included in my contract which is an easy way to show a client that Existing Conditions Surveying, for example, is not included in the basic fee but instead billed out at $1.50 per square foot of surveyed space.

You have much to think about when you're getting your firm up and running, the AIA documents will serve you well as a starting point. As your practice scales and you learn more about the clientele you serve, you can hire an attorney specializing in construction law to develop a contract custom-tailored to your business.

The AIA contracts are for sale individually or by annual subscription and you can easily review them in PDF form before purchasing. You're not required to be a member of the AIA to use their contracts. Their Documents on Demand program allows you to purchase and download the contract of your choice immediately for about $30 (USD). These are single-use documents, but the cost can either be passed along to your client as a reimbursable expense or written off as a business expense – it's up to you.

If you'd like to develop your own contract, you should always consult a construction law attorney. This isn't a DIY project you need professional help. If you're a new member of the AIA, you can subscribe to their LegaLine Service at a special introductory rate (as of 2015 it was: 3 months for $175 or 6 months for $300). At these rates, it may make sense to join the AIA for the access alone. Legal fees are costly, but far less expensive than paying for a legal defense of a poorly written contract.

Fees. Your contract codifies your compensation terms. You probably have already had some discussion with your client during the interview process about your typical fee structure, but the contract makes the terms explicit. There are many fee structures to consider, let's look at a few.

Fixed Fee (Stipulated Sum): A negotiated, fixed dollar amount which includes all your direct personnel expenses (if you're a sole-proprietor that's only you), any of your consultant's fees, your profit, and your overhead (the cost of doing business, not necessarily attributable to the project).

I can almost guarantee that this is the type of contract your client will request.

This fee structure has hazards though. First, it's rare that everything about a project is known from the outset. Project scope, budget, and timelines are always changing. The design process itself will reveal new possibilities and opportunities, clients (and designers) reevaluate, reimagine, and change their minds – it's a natural part of an iterative process. How can you then be expected to assign a fee to a moving target?

Second, you're still in the process of figuring out what it takes to operate your business and produce all the work using your systems. You won't have an informed sense for what it takes to execute a project using your SOPs. You can't be expected to know this information yet, but if you guess too low (which is common) it could be an expensive lesson with this fee structure.

When everything is known about a project, a fixed fee rewards your efficient work processes and penalizes the inefficient ones. Time spent on the project correlates directly with your profit margin. More time = less profit. This formula leaves little room for error in estimation (unless you build in a contingency). It's also a disincentive to taking the time to get things right and pursue a variety of options. I also think it unfairly benefits the client. We're looking for a fair agreement, not a lopsided one. Fixing the fee is essentially a salary model of compensation for you. Given that most clients have never worked with an architect before, this can mean a lot of handholding without hope of financial remuneration.

If you opt for this kind contract, you'll need to diligently account for any changes in the scope of work along the way. If the goal of the project is to have a happy client, renegotiating contracts every few weeks stands in direct opposition to that goal. I dislike the idea of having to repeatedly renegotiate a contract with a client as things change and your client is likely to resent this process as much as you do. They'll feel as though you're nickel-and-diming them and you'll feel taken advantage of because you're giving them more and more without compensation. Renegotiation is an absolute requirement with this compensation structure and it can be just plain difficult to do (not to mention time-consuming).

There is a place for the fixed fee model as we'll see.

Percentage of Construction Cost: Typically ranging from 5 to 20 percent (or more) of the cost of construction, this structure has a different set of liabilities. You'll need to carefully quantify the costs that make up the "construction cost." Some things to think about are: site development costs, utility installation, permitting, hard costs, engineering, and other soft costs.

Recognize that including or excluding one or more of the above items from the "construction cost" could result in wildly different compensation packages for you. My advice is to take a similar approach to this as a contractor would: if you have a hand in coordinating it, you should include that in the "cost of construction" calculation so you're compensated for it.

Owners are usually less fond of this approach than the fixed fee. That's because as the price of a home escalates so does the design fee. This can breed resentment when specific line items of the rising costs are looked at honestly. For example, in reality it takes little more for you to accommodate a $10,000 professional cooking range in your design than it does one that costs $2,000. Yet you're entitled to an extra $1200 in fee (assuming a 15 percent average fee). This isn't always the case, but often it is.

As the scope (and cost) increases so does the fee, which eliminates the need to renegotiate every time it changes as with the fixed fee. But there are two key elements necessary for this to work well:

> 1 – The designer must be an expert in the real cost of construction locally and be willing to consistently update it as it relates to the changing scope of work.

> 2 – The client must be forthright and honest with their budget and program requirements.

You can imagine that without either of those two components, the expectations of either party regarding the costs involved, will be incorrect and unmet. Here's an example to illustrate the flaw. Let's say a client comes to you looking for a 5,000 square foot home, you tell them it costs $200 per square foot to build in your area and they say fine. Inside they're thinking, "We can do it for $100 a square foot; we have before." From a budget standpoint, your client actually has only enough to build 2,500 square feet. If you proceed with assumption that they have the funds to construct the 5,000 square foot home, you risk absorbing a substantial redesign cost when the bids come back at double what they were expecting. Turning a 5,000 square foot home into a 2,500 square foot home isn't possible without a complete redesign. I can tell you from experience that people always think their project will cost less than you tell them it will. It's imperative that the budget and program size be aligned before doing any design work.

You can address redesign contingencies specifically in your percentage of construction cost contract. If you don't and a client decides to reduce the scope of work - along with it reducing the size and total budget - you'll be working for free (assuming you met the project objectives as outlined in the contract). You never want to end up in the position of redesigning something that's 'more affordable' for free.

You can start to appreciate how the competing needs of the designer and owner can foster tense relations with this fee structure. An architect working in good faith to reduce the overall cost of construction actually reduces the overall compensation they're eligible to receive. And an owner who wants a more expensive countertop material is penalized for selecting something that requires no more effort to design and detail.

For these reasons, homeowners and pros often avoid using the percentage of construction as their principal agreement.

Hourly Rate: This will be your client's least favorite option and it will probably be your preferred option. Despite your client's objections, it's quite common (and fair) to begin new projects with an hourly fee structure, especially when the exact scope of work hasn't been defined.

The hourly rate is a function of your geographic area, prevailing rates, your experience level and a host of detailed mathematical formulas. Endeavor to understand each of these as best you can, but also know that some of this information will be unknowable to you.

This means you'll have to take an honest guess at a reasonable rate that balances many business-related factors and what you think it will take to secure the commission. Don't forget that your rate needs to encompass all of the taxes, fees, and costs associated with keeping your business operational and what you think it will take to actually do the job. Forget about the rate you used when you were moonlighting. Or at least double it.

People expect to pay professional rates for professional services. If you tell someone you're charging $40 per hour, they'll tie a certain perception and quality to the service you offer. Higher rates command more respect and demand you deliver a higher quality service. If you're doing high-end home design, your rate should mirror your clientele's expectations. Commercial interior fit-out work is different, as are schools and so on. I can't tell you what to charge, only to make sure you've thought about how it correlates with your experience level and your ideal client avatar.

To better help guide your thinking about hourly rates, here are a few guideposts I used along the way.

-There are roughly 2,000 work hours in a year.

-As a principal, the most you can expect to work on billable time is 50%; the other 50% goes into business operations.

-Plan for half of your first year's revenue will go to tax (Federal, State and Local).

This means that if you're able to work a full year's time, you'll bill for only 1,000 hours. In your first year, you'll be extremely fortunate to get there, but it's a good goal. If we assume a hypothetical billing rate of $100 per hour and multiply it by 1,000 hours we get $100,000. Not bad for your first year's revenue. Depending on where you practice and your effective tax-rate, as a self-employed business owner, expect to net about $50,000 of that. Before you get too depressed, remember that your business expenses are deductible and will reduce your tax liability. If you structure your business wisely you can avoid paying more tax than necessary. This is meant to give you a basic idea a general roadmap to help you choose a billing rate; your tax situation will vary so talk with an accountant.

This underscores the correlation between your billable rate and your annual income. You're a professional and you should charge as any professional would. Keeping the lights on and your business operational has real-world costs, it's reasonable to add those up and pass them along in your billing rate to the clients who hire you.

You'll soon realize that even if you're working as much as you possibly can, your income will be limited in scale by two things. One is your billing rate and the other is your time.

Now, scaling may be a more attractive option to you. If you can leverage an employee's billing rate, you can increase your revenues and your profit margin. Adding an employee to help with drafting can boost your net earnings in a profound way. If you pay an employee $40 per hour to draft for you, the rate you bill your client might be $80 per hour. You've just increased your own effective billing rate by a significant margin and the bonus is that their billing percentage will be closer to 85% or 90% because they're drafting not running the business – that's your job. Adding employees has a different set of costs, which shouldn't be underestimated, but the advantages of the hourly rate at scale start to become clear.

Hourly rates can be a difficult thing to sell to a client. Clients prefer known, quantifiable costs (like the fixed fee), of course, we all do. Hourly billing for a service that client has no prior experience with can mean your client is surprised by a larger than expected monthly bill. This means you'll definitely hear about it. When it comes time to generate invoices for work completed this can lead to a struggle for you to define what you'll actually invoice. Designers work long hours, which result in large bills, which leads to you second-guessing whether you should bill for the time you actually put into the project.

You, the design professional, benefit from this fee structure because you're paid for every hour you work. Because your profit is built into your rate, you're covering your expenses and making money for each hour you invoice. But efficiency in an hourly contract isn't rewarded like a fixed fee arrangement. Designing things faster and more efficiently only results in fewer billable hours – the spoils go to your client, not you.

If you think this is a good structure for you, you can offset some of the objections your clients will raise by removing some of the uncertainty. One way to do this is to tie your overall fee to a percentage of the cost of construction and match each phase of the work to a fixed percentage of that fee. Here's the step-by-step process for doing that.

Let's assume we've programmed a new home to 3,000 square feet and assumed a $250 per square foot construction cost, netting a $750,000 estimated construction budget. The next step is to estimate the design fee, which we'll tie to a percentage of the cost of construction. Typical fees range from 5 to 25 percent; we'll use 15 percent for this example. This means the estimated fee would be $112,500.

The total fee ($112,500) is then subdivided into each phase of the work. Take the fee per phase and divide it by the billing rate, which will net an estimated number of hours per phase to guide the design and production process. Your percentages per phase may vary, but the table here is a good starting point.

Predesign	Billed Hourly.	
Schematic Design (20%)	$22,500	(180 hours @ $125/hour)
Design Development (20%)	$22,500	(180 hours @ $125/hour)
Construction Documents (35%)	$39,375	(315 hours @ $125/hour)
Bidding/Negotiation (5%)	$5,625	(45 hours @ $125/hour)
Construction Observation (20%)	$22,500	(180 hours@ $125/hour)
Total Fee Estimate:	$112,500	(900 hours @ $125/hour)

The fee total of 900 hours should be verified against the hours you expect to invest in-total for the project. If you're working 50 percent of your time on billable work, divide 900 (hours) by 20 (actual billable hours worked per week). This leaves 45 weeks to complete the entire project from start to finish. This helps with your internal scheduling when you're deciding what you can and can't take on for work.

The benefit of structuring the fee this way in a proposal is that the client has the information they need to budget for your fee along the way. They also have a rough schedule of how long each phase will take to complete and you'll still be paid for every hour that you work on the project. This is also a form of price anchoring, which we discussed earlier. Clients see and remember the numbers you give them. They'll know from the outset that a schematic design for their size project will roughly cost $22,500 to generate. This chart quantifies an abstract hourly fee by offering actual numbers. If you happen to come in lower than your estimated fee, you'll come away as a hero.

Hourly billing forces clients to be more efficient in their decision making because they realize that indecision and waffling has a quantifiable cost. Phone calls and meetings are usually fewer, more direct and to the point. For those clients who have the funds to indulge themselves in a more drawn-out process, you'll be able to bill them for the time you spend together.

If your fee percentages are worked out correctly and things proceed as expected with your client, your billable totals will closely correlate with the initial proposal. If you consistently exceed or fall short for one or more phases of the estimated overall fee, alter the percentages in your template to more accurately reflect the reality of your process. For example, I'm quite efficient in production but I like to dedicate more time to schematic design. I had to adjust my percentages for the phases to reflect this reality.

Two distinct disadvantages to this as a proposal structure emerge. When a client sees the fee breakdown they always look for ways to save money. They can treat the breakdown as if it were an à la carte menu where they can choose to do some but not all phases. This is a problem of education and one you can address in the lead-up to the proposal and the indoctrination in your working methodology.

The second disadvantage is that clients assume the numbers per phase are fixed, not-to-exceed maximums. I'm careful to point out in my proposal, using bolded, capitalized text in red that, "ALL WORK IS BILLED ON AN HOURLY BASIS." It sounds ridiculous, but it's a handy reference point when a client is quibbling over an invoice.

Other fee arrangements exist that capitalize on the benefits of the hourly agreement without adopting it for every phase of the work as we'll see in the next section.

Hybrid Fee: Balancing the assets and liabilities of each of the above structures is the aim of the hybrid fee arrangement. When a client balks at an hourly fee or you, the design professional, can't fix a fee for work you don't know the full scope and scale of, you'll need a more nuanced approach.

One method is to begin the work on an hourly basis from Predesign (programming, site and code analysis, etc.) through Design Development. When the specifics of a project are unknown this arrangement benefits you, the designer. Hourly fees are an incentive for the client to define their project goals efficiently and to select a schematic design direction.

You'll be compensated for the time it takes to fully understand the project scope and you'll also be able to see how your client operates. Take note of how quickly they're able to make decisions, how they respond to your design presentations, and their need to explore a variety of options.

As the scope, budget, schematic design direction and your client's working habits are better defined, you'll have a better idea about exactly what it will take to complete the remaining parts of the project. It's then much easier to fix a fee for the Construction Documents phase. That's a phase where you control most of the variables and can benefit from an efficient workflow. When the project enters the Construction Observation phase you might transition back to an hourly fee where your time inputs are directly compensated.

The needs of your client and the selected contractor are highly variable during the Construction Observation phase so an hourly structure makes sense. Site meetings, specific client requirements, sub-trades and schedule are all variables out of your control; fixing a fee would be a poor choice.

Another possible fee structure is to begin work as above with an hourly fee for the Predesign and Schematic Design phases – where you're defining the scope of work. Once a schematic design has been selected, the intermediate phases can be tied to an estimated percentage of construction cost. Adding a contingency to the construction estimate of 5 to10 percent is necessary to account for the unknowns that will be defined as you develop the design (finishes, systems, details, etc.)

This arrangement benefits the client offering them a fixed fee for the bulk of the work. The contract doesn't require constant renegotiation because the fee adjusts with the cost of construction and changes in scope. And the design professional is more easily able to fix a price because there's a defined schematic design.

Fixed fees inherently shift the risk from the client to the design professional. I happen to think designers and architects already own a disproportionate share of the risk in any given project so for my business I won't accept any more. If you have a client who insists on fixing a fee, you can simply remind them that this exposes you to more risk and add a premium to account for it. Make it worth your while.

Other Contract Items

Reimbursable Expenses. Outside of the fee discussed above, reimbursable expenses are hard costs for items directly attributable to the project, which you'll be asking your client to reimburse you for. These can vary depending on the specifics of a project but are generally items like:

> Prints
> Reproduction costs
> Travel Expenses (mileage, tolls, airfare, and lodging)
> Postage
> Permitting Fees

For small projects, close to your office, it may not make sense to actually invoice for these because they take time and resources to track. You'll have to decide whether the time it takes to do so is worth it. Even if you consider these items incidental, you'll want a provision in your contract to cover you in case they escalate for reasons beyond your control. The contract is there to protect you so be sure to leave open the option to bill for them.

Scope of Work. Clearly state what you'll be doing, how you'll be doing it and if necessary what you won't be doing in your contract. For example, if the garage will remain unaltered say, "The garage will not be considered and is not a part of this proposal." Be sure to spell out the deliverables for a project too. If your client is expecting one thing and you're expecting to provide another, that's a problem of communication. Saying, "Physical models, computer models and renderings are considered an 'additional service' available at additional cost on request," makes it explicit. If you haven't included a fee menu of services, you should state it elsewhere in the agreement.

An unambiguous scope of work benefits all parties. From a client's perspective they know what the deliverables are. If they want service above and beyond those deliverables, they'll know exactly what it will cost as an additional service. From the design professional's perspective a clear scope of work keeps you on task and ensures you're fairly compensated for the work you've proposed to do.

The scope definition ties more professional service with more compensation – that's the goal. This helps you stay profitable too, you can't afford to throw in a 3D model of their space as a favor, there's a real cost associated with producing it. A profitable business can exert more influence in the world.

You'll be able to serve more people while supporting your family when your business remains viable and profitable.

Adding Value

When you're first developing fee proposals for your contract, resist paring down your fee to an absolute minimum. Remember that the bulk of the money in an architectural project is not in the design fee; it's in the construction of the physical work of architecture. A $70,000 architectural fee viewed as a stand-alone product can seem exorbitant. It's a large sum of money by any measure. But when viewed in the context of a $700,000 project it's an amazing value for your client.

Design professionals are responsible for choreographing the complex process of design and construction. You organize thoughts, ideas, sites and budgets into a coherent whole that carefully balances your client's needs and wants. You can minimize construction delays, negotiate change orders; you'll design an efficient floor plan and modern building systems that use less energy. Your buildings are backed by knowledge of building science and best practices; they're prone to fewer failures and have lower maintenance costs. These are all of direct financial benefit to your client. That's real money back in their pockets.

Of course, there are the intangibles too; the things good design confers to one's comfort, aesthetic enjoyment and practical function of a home.

These are all reasons you shouldn't undervalue your services. When a client balks at the high cost of your design services you can feel confident in walking away. Someone fee shopping various design professionals is a client to be avoided; one your business can't afford to work with.

What works for me: The hourly method, diagrammed in detail above, is what I've found works best for my business. When it's presented in my proposal I always categorize the fee exactly as I've illustrated it. I keep a spreadsheet to track project fees by phase, which is all tied to construction cost. Early on, the construction cost is an estimate developed by me based on local square footage costs. As we receive pricing feedback from a contractor, I'll replace my estimate with theirs. For those clients who request it or who consistently balk at my invoices, I'll send them the fee track with each monthly invoice.

8 | Finances

"Anybody who wants more money, a better job, or a bigger house is ultimately just wishing for a new set of anxieties."
-Merlin Mann

When starting your design firm financial concerns will weigh heavily on you. Although start-up costs are the first costs you'll have to address, they're actually much less important to the health of your business than your overall financial structure – your accounting, bookkeeping and tax strategy.

Financing basic living expenses as your business grows from no clients, to one, to many, sits at the top of a long list of concerns. For me, financial uncertainty, was (and still is) the most stressful aspect of building a business. If there isn't a plan in place for covering your basic living expenses from the beginning, the inevitable lean times may force you out of business altogether.

You may feel pressure to accept work that is a poor fit or for a less-than-ideal client to pay your monthly bills. When you accept projects that are a poor fit out of financial desperation it's not only bad for you and your business, it's also unfair to your client.

Giving up a consistent paycheck requires a big shift in your attitude toward your personal finances. Your job in the past acted like an ATM, every two weeks you could be assured that it would top up again and you could spend at will. Now, you're responsible for deciding whether you'll draw funds from the business regularly - like a paycheck - or whether you'll use it to capitalize the business, invest in equipment or competitions, advertising or supplies. The regular paycheck is a relic of your past; you'll adopt a new means of paying yourself from the profits of the business.

So how can you relieve the stress, minimize the hardship and still go pro?

Trim Expenses. If you diligently evaluate and pare down your current expenses, the steps that follow will be much easier. If you don't already have one, develop a budget listing all your current monthly expenses and revenues. You don't have to ruthlessly eliminate everything that makes you happy, the budgeting process is meant to uncover and make known everything that you spend money on in a given month. When looked at in its totality you can make an honest assessment and decide whether the expenditure is offering a good value exchange.

Carefully managing and budgeting your money will leave you less time to actually spend it too. The leaner you can live, the longer you can keep your business afloat. But you still need income to live, so in the next step you're going to build a runway.

Runway (Your Savings). Your personal savings account is your runway. It's up to you to decide how long a runway you want to construct. Recommendations I found when starting out ranged from as little as three months to as much a year's worth of living expenses. Have you ever totaled an entire year's worth of living expenses? It's a large number. If you wait until you're able to save a full year's runway you'll never make the leap.

I think a good starting point is 6 months which is still a substantial sum. When you're out of runway you get a job. This idea itself can be a particularly motivating factor; it was for me. I was determined never to be an employee again. When I was paid for a job, I was sure to first allocate the taxes due on the income and then use the balance to rebuild my runway up to six months of living expenses. So long as I had six months of living expenses banked, I was confident I could drum up enough work in the interim to keep the business operational. I still use the runway concept in my business today.

Here's another option. Why not build your business while you're still working for someone else and reduce or eliminate the need for a runway altogether?

Working Spouse. If your spouse earns enough to support the family, starting your firm is far less risky. It doesn't, however, mean you can spend with impunity or that you don't need a budget. It still makes good sense to follow the discipline the above steps enforce, but having the freedom to build your business without worry about how you're going to feed your family is much more enjoyable and your missteps don't carry with them extreme financial burden.

It can sap motivation, though, which is a real concern. The drive to figure things out that financial pressure brings to bear is good and bad. There should still be accountability built-in to your financial structure. Your business must make a profit, which is to say, your revenues must exceed your expenses. In fact, the IRS demands it as a condition of you doing "business" and not merely dabbling in a hobby. You must post a profit in at least three of the past five years to be counted as a legitimate business in the eyes of the IRS.

To be a successful business you'll need to consistently build your revenue streams and remain profitable. Having a second household income provides more latitude to make this possible, but it doesn't relieve the responsibility to deliver on your brand's promise.

Debt Zero. I recommend you run a debt-zero business, which means one that doesn't take on loans or financing. Debt is a substantial drag on the viability and profitability of any business – new or established. Debt limits the freedom you have to choose the projects that are right for your brand because you'll choose work based on need rather than fit. It also cuts into your profit margin, reducing it by the APR (annual percentage rate) of the loan.

Business loans vary a great deal depending on the lending institution and loan amount. To borrow amounts less than $100,000 you'll be repaying the loan at an interest rate between 7-8%; assuming you qualify for one. Without a proven record of past earnings, a bank is unlikely to roll the dice on your business venture.

You're in luck though, a design business can be run with very little on hand to start and expenses almost always have lower cost or free alternatives. What about your workspace; your studio? Rent is a financial drag, work from home if possible. What about expensive design software? There are many free, or very low-cost, options we'll discuss in the chapter in Chapter 12. How about a company car? Use your own vehicle and track the mileage for tax purposes.

A salary is one expense that doesn't have a less costly counterpart. Taking on employees and salaries will almost surely require a line of credit to smooth out the bumps between invoicing and payment. Access to working capital when you have employees is useful; however, early on you don't want a regular loan payment to add to your financial burdens. This should confirm a decision to begin as a sole proprietor or enter into a partnership where the risk is shared among equals. Taking on a salaried employee is no small responsibility. They have families to feed and living expenses too - they're counting on you for their income.

If you need employees to do the work for you, consider hiring freelance or independent contractors. Drafting, 3D modeling, engineering, even office administration work can be outsourced with relative ease. In fact, virtual assistants represent an entirely new emerging economy because people like you are taking control of their own destiny. These services are on-demand expenses, meaning you'll incur them only when there's work in the pipeline and they'll be paid with receivables not a bank loan. You can even mark up their invoices to account for time spent managing your virtual assistants, which means you'll be even more profitable.

Imagine for a moment taking a loan or line of credit to cover any one of these large cash outlays or recurring expenses. Loans capture the first dollars of your revenues each month. On day one of the calendar month, you're already behind. Not a good feeling is it? Consider the taxi driver who leases a cab in New York City. Typical drivers spend most of their day just trying to break even. They need enough fares to repay the company who owns the car for the opportunity to drive the car to make a living.

With a business loan, you'll be on a monthly cycle and slightly more removed from the cab driver's daily repayment cycle, but the example illustrates the real burden debt can have on your freedom to make strategic decisions. Cab drivers don't choose their fares based on where they want to drive. They take any fare that comes along.

The equivalent of taking every fare for you may mean working on commercial interiors, or for the impossible-to-please client who speaks poorly about you when the project is over. Or it could mean partnering with a developer who doesn't pay you because the project never received financing.

Rejecting financing is a conservative strategy and it means your business won't scale as quickly as those with more capital. Running a lean-startup means growth is funded with cash not debt. As your business revenues increase, you'll have access to cash to reinvest in the business. It may mean you can upgrade your studio, or buy new furniture; purchase a new laptop or maybe a laser cutter. Likewise, when you hit a slow patch and the revenues aren't there you won't grow the business.

If your roadmap for your firm means scaling beyond a few people, you'll need a plan to leverage financing or outside investment at the points of scale along the way. Those are steps outside the scope of this book and require a much different attitude toward borrowing and debt.

Accounting and Bookkeeping. Never having taken a business accounting class in any of my years of schooling, I was at a loss when it came to accounting. I knew I needed to keep track of expenses and maintain a set of books, but I didn't know where to start. I began by scheduling meetings with and talking to accountants. The initial consult was free, I was essentially interviewing them. They helped lay the groundwork for my weekly accounting and helped me discern what I needed to track for tax purposes.

I recommend that you hire a professional to guide you through this process to get your books in order properly from the beginning. You don't need to meet weekly; perhaps only quarterly right before your taxes are due. Ask other local small businesses for a recommendation. An accountant's advice is worth the small expenditure (it's also a tax write-off). It will free you to work on the parts of your business where your skills can be better leveraged, design or marketing for example.

If you want to stay with the lean-startup model, after the initial meeting with an accountant transition over to an online bookkeeping service – QuickBooks, Xero, Harvest, Wave, or Freshbooks. They're easy to set up, link to your bank account, and ensure transactions are all logged correctly. Some are free, some are paid.

Invoicing and Payment Terms. Your contract should precisely spell out the terms of payment and any penalties for nonpayment. For some reason, the design disciplines are notorious for attracting slow paying clients. Whether it's because design lacks the immediacy of a mechanical repair for a car, or there's just less perceived value, we often find ourselves waiting for payment from our clients.

I recommend sending all invoices as "Due Upon Receipt." Small businesses don't have the working capital to provide a temporary line of credit for their clients. Before sending out the first invoice for a new project, it's not uncommon for you to have been working on it for many weeks prior. If you send an invoice with terms, "Net 30 days," that would mean the time it takes to convert a worked hour into cash would be more than two months. Work the hour, send the design to the client, the client reviews, invoice 2 weeks later, 30 days net. That's a long time.

My typical process is something like this:

There's an initial point of contact, a phone call or e-mail and assuming that goes well we'll arrange for a visit to the project site. Next, I'll develop a proposal and send it to the client. At this point I've already invested between one and four weeks into the process.

The client will review the contract and usually sign it without too much back and forth. Overall this adds between one and three weeks to the process, depending on how schedule-driven the project is. After signing the proposal, I'll commit to a start date and relay that to the client. It's only after this point that I'll start logging billable hours as I begin predesign, programming, site analysis, code review and eventually schematic design.

It a substantial time investment between the initial phone call and the time when the first invoice is actually sent, never mind paid. This is the natural cycle of design business though and it makes sense to seek projects that reward this investment asymmetrically. That is, your fee should reflect the effort and professional service you're offering. It should make you question too whether it makes sense to pursue many little projects or a few larger ones. The same amount of effort is required of each with regards to lead conversion, client management and invoicing. Why not opt for fewer, better paying jobs than many smaller ones?

Whichever path you choose, your contract should make it clear that payment is expected promptly. To incentivize prompt payment you may offer a discount (no more than 5%) for clients who can agree to set terms. Be explicit when describing the terms of this arrangement. You wouldn't want to discount your subconsultant's fees for them or be left with the responsibility for paying them an extra 5% out of your pocket.

Retainers can mitigate some of the risk you assume early in a project. A retainer is like a deposit made by the client to you when they sign the contract. Typically, they're for values between 5 and 15% of the design fee. The cash amount is held by you for the duration of the project. At the end of the project, the sum is deducted from your final invoice. It's not a prepayment of your first month's fee. Clients and designers alike often confuse this so be sure the contract clearly says that the retainer serves to hold the client's place in line and as a credit against the final payment due. If the retainer were used to pay the first invoice you'd be right back where you started, behind the client, billing to catch up.

Choosing whether a retainer is right for you is a personal decision based on the cash flow of your business. The retainer can make doing the work initially a little easier and less stressful as it provides a cash input in what's usually a lean time.

Another option to consider is a deposit system broken out by project phase. The client submits a fixed deposit for a defined set of deliverables broken down by project phase. The designer works through the fee and when it's close to being consumed, the client is notified. The fund is either refilled or work pauses. Again, this prevents you from getting behind on your fees.

It helps to know your client before committing to a payment structure. For example, developers have a reputation for working out fee agreements with designers contingent on project financing. Because much of their work is speculative, financing often falls through. Don't relinquish the terms of your payment to forces beyond your control.

When a client is late in paying you'll need to be disciplined about stopping work. Contact your client immediately and stop work. The first thing you want to learn is whether there's a reason they're not paying. Are they unhappy with what you've given them? Is there a dispute between spouses about the direction of the project? Is the budget an issue? Resolving problems in the field is a skill of yours that you'll rely on in client relations too. Work to find a resolution to the circumstances delaying payment. Let them know that not paying your bill doesn't solve the problem.

If the problem escalates, you can always hire a collection agency to help you recover payment and of course you can withhold deliverables or place a lien on their property. However, those are usually final decisions made when you and a client have irreconcilable differences. Your professional relationship will effectively end at that point.

Continuing to work based on a client's promise to pay is a real risk to the financial solvency of your business. I've worked for small firms who assumed losses in excess of $40,000 from clients who decided not to pay their bills. That's more than 300 hours of professional work! If payment doesn't arrive, stop work. It's really that simple.

For clients motivated by schedule, stopping work is usually enough to jump-start the payment process. It will quickly become clear to them that they're the ones responsible for delaying the project – not you. And for clients who aren't motivated by schedule, stopping work transfers the power back to you to choose which billable projects to prioritize in the meantime. Late payers always go to the back of the line in my business; the front of the line is reserved for early payers.

What works for me: Because my business accounting needs are relatively simple, I use Wave Accounting for all of my bookkeeping tasks. It's cloud-based, free, and it's easy to use. The software is linked to my business bank account and automatically imports transactions. From there I'm able to categorize the expenses, create invoices and run any reports I may need. Although I don't use all of these, the program has modules for: invoicing, billing, accounting, payroll, receipts, transactions and reports.

Invoices in Wave aren't linked a time tracking module, which makes it a manual process. I track billable hours in a separate program (Toggl) and create invoices in Wave. The invoices can be emailed directly to the client from within the program and are fully customizable to include your logo and any tracking codes you use to bill. The lack of integration with an overall project budget may be problematic for your business. If I had many projects to invoice each month, I'd probably look for a more integrated solution like ArchiOffice, which combines time tracking, projects budgeting and invoicing in one package. I use an Excel spreadsheet to track overall billings against the project budget.

At the end of each quarter, assuming one uses the bank integrations and categorizes the transactions correctly, the prepopulated reports deliver all the financial information one would ever need to close out the books. Wave also offers a network of accountants to help you as needed for a small fee.

Free and cloud-based were the two most important things to me as I was choosing accounting software. I was able to accept some of the limitations of the program (lack of time tracking and no cash-accounting option) in exchange for these terms. Should I decide I want to transition to a different program, I'm able to export my data.

Taxes. Assuming your business has earned a profit during the year; taxes will consume a large portion of that profit. Chapter 2 explained the tax system in detail so you're already familiar with the scope of costs. Remember, your business structure, personal income and overall revenues all contribute to your overall tax liability.

Year one can be tricky to figure out. When you set up the initial meeting with an accountant, be sure to note your previous year's AGI (Adjusted Gross Income) from your IRS form 1040. Ask the accountant how to plan for paying quarterly taxes based on that information.

You're responsible for one of two things when it comes to paying taxes without a penalty. You must either pay 100% of your previous year's tax liability or 90% of this year's tax due. This is helpful to know when you have a spouse bringing home a steady income. You can use their prior year's tax withholding and subtract from that from your prior year's tax due to arrive at a figure. Divide the remaining number by four and you'll see have an idea of what will be due each quarter. You'll have paid 100% of your prior year's tax.

Although I recommend this as a conservative strategy, many elect not to pay quarterly tax and choose to pay the penalty when filing their annual tax return in April. The penalties are actually quite low, but because it's a pay as you-go system you're certainly not playing by IRS rules.

Tax deadlines in the US are: January 15, April 15, June 15, and September 15. Don't forget you'll have to pay the Federal government and your individual State government separately.

You can automate your payments using the Federal site: www.eftps.gov/eftps, check with your State government's official site for their electronic tax payment system.

The tax system in the United States is a graduated tax meaning you pay a smaller percentage on the first dollars you earn than you do on your last dollar. The brackets are different for individuals and married couples. Detailed information on tax brackets is listed on the IRS website, but basically the first dollars you earn in the year will be taxed at 10%, the next at 15%, 25%, 38%, 33%, 35%, and 39.6% (2015 figures). If you're self-employed (i.e. - not a corporation) you'll need to also add your Social Security payment, which is fixed at 15.3% no matter what you earn.

What works for me: For my first year in business I calculated my Federal liability this way: 15.3% for Social Security payment, plus I knew my top tax bracket was 25%. That's 40% of my earnings in total due to the Federal government. For state tax liability, I used a percentage from my accountant to estimate my liability, which we calculated to be 8% (for Maine). So, for every dollar that I received in net revenues, I allocated 48-cents toward taxes. About a week before each quarter close, I would generate a P+L (profit and loss) report in my accounting software to arrive at a net quarterly revenue total (revenues minus expenses). I would multiply that total by 40% (Federal) and 8% (State) and schedule two electronic payments to withdraw the funds on the deadline date.

As you might imagine, I received a large refund, because I paid each quarter's tax at my top marginal tax rate of 25%. It was simpler, but the government benefited, keeping my dollars for the entire year. If you get more granular than this you can do much better, but it's a personal choice, I didn't want to end the year with a surprise tax bill.

You can either be very meticulous about generating your P&L report or you can use rough figures. By deducting your expenses (home office, mileage, etc.) at the end of each quarter, you can arrive at a very accurate tax payment due. I loosely follow this rule, deducting the business transactions in my accounting software throughout the quarter. These are items like professional dues, meals for clients, magazine subscriptions and various supply expenses. The software doesn't allow me to automatically itemize expenses related to my home office, which are significant, so I estimate and record these in a separate spreadsheet to calculate the tax due. If you're due to receive a refund on your annual return you'll have the option to turn that around and prepay your upcoming quarterly tax payment due on April 15th.

At the end of year one, you'll have a better idea of how to adjust your contributions for the following year.

9 | Studio Essentials

"We become what we behold. We shape our tools, and thereafter our tools shape us." - Marshall McLuhan

Finally, nine chapters in, we're getting around to discussing your studio space. You now know the reason we didn't start by feathering your studio nest in chapter one, because the foundations of your business were to establish your brand message, define your USP, and find clients who resonate with what you do best. Having completed the steps in the previous chapters you should have inquiries coming in and perhaps a few new projects on your boards. You also have a plan in place to rinse and repeat. It's time to focus on your studio.

Think of your studio as an extension of your brand. Where you choose to work, how you set it up, even what you choose to display and how you greet new clients into your workspace all refer back to your brand. Consider what practicing in a rented strip mall space or a small modern shed on your property might say about your brand? There's a real difference between those two options, right?

Location
Deciding where you'll physically locate your business is step one. The choice is essentially between renting a space and working from home. There's a delicate balance between your need to be seen as a professional in the world (i.e. - renting a space on Main Street), your revenues and your fixed expenses.

Your fixed expenses are one of the few things you control as a bootstrapped entrepreneur. The choice is simply a question of economics.

Spending money on a brand-new studio and paying for a highly visible location squanders one of your most powerful competitive advantages: your low overhead. From the previous chapter on finances you know that taking on debt at an early stage can stifle the growth potential of a new business and a monthly rent payment is debt that's owed at the beginning of each month. It's a financial ball and chain that may sink your business before you've had a chance to fully develop it.

You can instead choose to use that low overhead as a lever to grow your business, to reinvest in your own assets not others, and to be the best value in your market. Think of the savings on rent as lengthening your runway. Without a rent payment, there will be less pressure to accept work that isn't right for your brand too.

In school, your studio was probably your home away from home. Now, it may be *in* your home and I'd recommend that's where you start – by working from home.

Home Studio

While the choice to work from home is a conundrum for some, for others it's not a choice; it's simply required. Working from home capitalizes on the fact that you need a place to live no matter what you're doing. It also turns part of your monthly housing cost and expenses into a business related tax deduction. This means you already have most of the infrastructure necessary to turn pro and practice out of your existing space.

Using part of your home as a studio is an extremely low barrier to entry. Your primary goal with your new business is to secure work. Once you do that, you'll find a suitable place to do the work. I lust after the studio space that Renzo Piano has, sure, but he didn't start there and you won't either.

Thankfully in today's economy, working from home doesn't have the negative connotations it once did. More and more people are rejecting the standard office environment in favor of working from home and people have become more accepting of the home office as a legitimate place to conduct business.

You'll want to check with your local municipality to make sure you're allowed to operate a profit-generating business from your home. For sole proprietors this usually isn't a problem, but if you have any employees you may find some regulations standing in your way.

If you'll be welcoming clients into your home, you'll need to let your insurance company know this too. No one plans on accidents; they just happen. Protect yourself from being sued by a client slipping on your icy driveway with the proper insurance coverage.

Before you open your home office consider the following positives and negatives:

Advantages
-No commute. This means more time dedicated to creative work, your family and the things you enjoy doing other than driving to and from an office. It lowers your personal expenses and it's better for the environment too.

-Brand Message. You control how your client experiences your brand. It's a chance to showcase your design skills too.

-Tax benefits. Corporations can shift wages into rent payments for tax savings. For sole proprietors there's the home office deduction, which turns part of your personal expenses into tax savings. Mileage (and deductions) is tracked beginning in your driveway, not a remote office.

-Low overhead. Lower fixed expenses translate into a lower hourly rate, which means you can charge less and remain profitable.

-Flexible Hours. Your work life can adapt to changes in your home life more easily. You can fit work in at odd times or times that are overall better for your personal life.

-Convenience. It's thoroughly convenient to work when you want with a home office steps away.

Disadvantages
- Distractions. All the chores and daily tasks are right there staring at you. There's laundry to fold, dishes to clean, and a lawn to mow. Your home is full of distractions.

- No distinction between Work and Home. This can mean more overall hours dedicated to your work than when you were an employee working for someone else. Walking out of an office and commuting home is a clear boundary that a home office doesn't provide.

- Isolation. If you're an office of one, you'll have to reach out to others – online and in person to combat the loneliness of working alone. There's also the creative isolation of solo practice to contend with too. Finding a community of people in similar situations can help

- Space constraints. Small homes or apartments with limited space for dedicated work may force some of your living spaces to multitask. Try to dissociate work and play environments. Don't work from your couch if you can help it, mixing relaxation and work is mentally difficult to reconcile.

- No Public Presence. A real challenge you'll face is how to get the public to find you and recognize the legitimacy of your business. Brick and mortar locations have the advantage here. To counteract your diminished public presence you'll have to spend more marketing dollars to achieve similar results to your more publicly positioned competition. If you live in a remote location, a home office may be just too far removed to be practical.

Some disadvantages can be minimized through focused effort. You'll need to find new ways of socializing during the day to feel less isolated. You'll probably want to establish a daily routine to keep household distractions from negatively impacting your work. If you can consciously address some of the negatives, you'll find that you can position your home as a unique business card and advertisement for your services.

Embrace the idea that you don't need a standard storefront to convey what you do well. You can creatively leverage your home office space to tell your brand's story and to sell your potential client that you're a legitimate business in other ways.

Dedicated Space
If you've weighed the options and decided a home office is right for you; you're not alone. Some talented designers have and continue to work from a home office, included in that pool is the world-renowned Finnish architect Alvar Aalto who worked out of a home office.

If you can, find a place that's solely dedicated to your work, a place with a clear boundary. Creating a threshold between work and home is as much a mental game as a physical one. You'll condition yourself to do work when you're in the office and to set it aside when you leave.

Working from your couch or dining room table can be fine as a temporary solution, but they're places that have an established pattern of use in our minds. The couch is for relaxing, the dining table is for sharing a meal with your spouse or family. Don't underestimate the power these connections have on your psyche.

Dedicating space to your professional work makes sense. It establishes in the client's mind that you're a pro, not an amateur. It's the foundation for doing quality, focused work. You owe it to your clients and yourself.

You may be surprised to know that the government cares too. If you'll be using your home office as a deduction on your tax filing, be sure to familiarize yourself with the IRS rules governing it. Your home office must be your primary place of business and, to count toward the deduction, the space you use must be distinct and used only for business purposes. This means if your dining table doubles as family dining and client meeting spot (as it does for me) you can't count that square footage toward the deduction. If the table were solely used for business, then you could.

It's to your advantage to separate the space too. It makes the area calculation, as a percentage of your overall home's square footage much easier. The resulting percentage is the figure you'll use to determine the amount of your home's expenses – heat, plowing, maintenance, taxes, utilities – that are assigned to the business.

Note: The home office tax deduction is essentially a deferred government loan. You're getting a break on your business tax obligations, but sooner or later the IRS will get paid. If you sell a home that includes a home office which has previously leveraged the home office tax deduction, the government "recaptures" the deferred payments in the tax year of the sale. Talk to an accountant about whether this makes sense for your situation.

Outbuildings. If you have an existing outbuilding to repurpose or a plan to construct a new small structure on your property, the home office can be even more attractive. This approach can address many of the disadvantages noted above and it ably meets the IRS criteria for separate and distinct.

Here are some advantages you may not have considered:

1. Privacy. As close as you'll probably become with your clients, they're not family. Welcoming clients into a dedicated space that's not your home inserts some professional distance between you and may actually be more comfortable for both parties. The importance of this will be revealed the first time you have an uncomfortable exchange with an unhappy client in your home. It's hard to divorce yourself from those interactions when they happen in your living space. It's also difficult not to view them as more personal than they really are because they're occurring in your home - your personal sanctuary.

If you have employees, the separate outbuilding protects your privacy in other and even more meaningful ways.

2. Convenience. A home office demands that your house remains well kempt and organized all the time. When a client visits you'll probably have to do some extra tidying and cleaning. Depending on your situation this can be more or less work. But in time you'll tire of this as a preface to any client meeting, I can guarantee it.

With a separate outbuilding, you'll be responsible for cleaning up after yourself and your work habits. In theory, this should be less work, but if your brand message is more Jackson Pollack than Tadao Ando then you may have to do nothing at all.

3. Mental preparation. When I used to commute to and from work I had time to prepare mentally for the day ahead and time to leave it behind in the evening. The physical and mental separation provided a clear boundary. Working from home that's harder to do, but even adding just a few steps between home and office can help immensely in rewiring your brain to working mode.

4. Taxes. A stand-alone structure housing your office is not only easy to assign expenses to but it's easy to defend in the case of an audit. If you're a corporation, you can choose to take a smaller (yet still competitive and reasonable) wage and shift that pay toward covering the rent (paid to you) for the outbuilding's use. This is an effective, and perfectly legal, way to save on the amount of employment tax the corporation has to pay.

5. Storefront. A stand-alone building can be the storefront you couldn't afford otherwise. If you design it, it can also be a showcase of your design talents.

If you're a design business that relies on retail sales as part of your income, it's likely that a home office won't fulfill all your needs out of the gate. But you can begin with one and devise a transition plan to move you from home to storefront by reinvesting your revenues as they become appropriate. Better yet, sell digitally and let others handle the product fulfillment for you (Fulfillment by Amazon is an excellent option).

Equally, if you can't work from home or the disadvantages far outweigh the advantages, you'll need to search for space to rent. Seek out coworking spaces first. That fits best with the lean start-up model and the cost will be much lower than committing to a year (or longer) lease for a dedicated office rental. Coworking spaces leverage shared resources and can provide the support and socialization you won't have working from home.

If coworking isn't for you either, then you'll want to contact a realtor to investigate the local commercial rental market. They can quickly give you an understanding of the actual costs and terms of the properties available in your area. You'll also get an idea of what's available in your price range. The scope of these negotiations extends beyond the mission of this book, which is aimed at getting you started quickly with as little financial risk as possible.

Outfitting Your Studio (The Essentials)
Your basic set of tools won't vary too much whether you work from home or a remote space. Fundamentally, you need only a few things to get started: a phone, a laptop, a website, a place to sketch and design, and a space to conduct meetings. Maybe a place to plug-in a coffeepot would be good too.

Computer Hardware. Lean start-ups will repurpose an existing machine, but if that isn't possible purchase a new laptop. The mobility a laptop offers means it can function as a mobile office, a presentation and production tool, and you can just as easily work from your dining table as you can from your drafting table. If you pair it with a large monitor, you can also use it for presentations to check drawings on screen rather than printing them.

Software. With so many specialized considerations for design and production software I've devoted an entire chapter (12) to it. It's essential reading.

Furniture. You'll want at a minimum a desk or large table to work at, preferably one that's big enough to accommodate your computer hardware and the design tools you regularly use. You'll want a table to spread out drawing sets on, a table dedicated to meetings, and a few bookshelves to hold your reference library. Here again, lean start-ups will find and repurpose existing furniture or track down affordable options from IKEA or thrift stores.

Phone. A landline is fine, you can even use VOIP if you have a fast Internet connection, but I advocate a cell phone, preferably a smart phone. With the right combination of apps, a smart phone rivals a computer in its everyday utility. It's an expensive item, and violates the lean start-up mindset, but a smart phone is required equipment in any entrepreneur's arsenal. And, while you can't write-off your home phone as a business expense, you can write-off a percentage of your cell phone, which offsets some of the recurring monthly cost. For tax purposes I assign 90% of my cell charges to the business.

Internet. As discussed before, the Internet is your gateway to marketing your services to the entire world. You'll need it to manage your web presence and you may come to rely on it for phone service, Skype call, or Google+ Hangouts.

Plotter or Printer. Your lean-self can probably get by using a local repro service like FedEx Office (formerly Kinko's) or Staples in the beginning. You might even consider going paperless early on. If you're doing residential work, an 11x17 printer may suffice.

At some point though, you'll probably trade cost for convenience and purchase a basic large format plotter, if only because it's easier printing things in-house when you need them (or at the last minute).

When you decide to purchase be sure to check the cost of the consumables like ink and print heads, which can really add up over time. Dependable large-format plotter can be purchased for around $1,000 USD. You'll also need a stand or large table to place it on.

I purchased my plotter immediately after the contract was signed on my first large commission. Now, I'm able to use it to generate some side revenue too printing sets for local contractors at $1 per square foot of printed media ($6 per 24X36 sheet). You're an entrepreneur, right?

Office Supplies. Pens, pencils, tracing paper, folders, Post-Its, paperclips – you know best what's required for you to do the work. Make a list and keep track of your expenditures. All the accouterments you can attribute to earning income are considered business expenses by the IRS.

Meeting space. Every practice differs in its need to meet with clients, contractors, sales representatives and consultants. Determine the amount of meeting space you'll need up front and have a plan in place to address it.

If most of your work is renovations or interior fit-outs, you can probably use the client's site and home to hold meetings. In fact, there are advantages from a design standpoint to conducting meetings in the actual space. New construction isn't as simple. You can't productively meet with a client on their undeveloped lot to review your designs.

Using your home is great if you can make it work. If not, find a coffee shop that could work, rent a meeting room in a hotel or find a local coworking space. Recognize that all of these are situations where you don't control the environmental variables, choose wisely.

Many clients also want to see the space where you work – where the magic happens. Consistently meeting in a coffee shop can project an air of unprofessionalism; that you're somehow less committed to professional results. It may not be true, but it only matters what your client thinks of it.

When you bring clients into your work space, your studio, you're selling them on your process and showing them that what you do is unique. This can be packaged and sold as an exclusive service and you can capitalize on their desire to be a part of that with a comparable (premium) fee.

In general, people can appreciate the clutter of the design process and actually expect a certain messiness when viewing a designer's workspace. For many it's an enriching experience to visit a studio overflowing with work in progress, sketches and cardboard models. The design process can lend you that extra bit of credibility that a client needs as reassurance that you're the right person for the job.

Reference Library. Your book collection may be dwindling as digital media takes hold, but I still have an affinity for physical books. A designer's library can speak to a client too. Displaying one's collection of books plainly shows your influences and tastes without blatantly stating them.

During client meetings, it's helpful to pull relevant books from my collection to illustrate ideas or options. Also included in this collection are inspirational books from photographers, sculptors, graphic designers, industrial archaeology, graphic novels, and short stories. These items speak to who I am as a person and I think clients appreciate knowing that other things in life inform my work as an architect.

When it comes to purely technical reference materials, things like code standards, graphic conventions, and product literature; I keep that collection pruned to a minimum. Most of these can be found online where they will always be up to date and accurate. Certain materials I find easier to navigate in hard copy form; things like window and door catalogs and those I keep nearby.

Sample Library. This may or may not speak to you, but for my work physical samples offer pure inspiration. They inform my design process and they're at the heart of who I am as an architect. Handing a client a sample of fractured slate or raw concrete to compare the feel, and weight and sense the color – there's no substitute for that kind of experience. Comparing material palettes and convincing someone of a particular design is made easier by having the raw materials of building nearby.

I never seem to have enough room for samples and they're heavy and bulky. I find using industrial rolling shelving units work well for storing and displaying samples and I limit myself to a certain size to keep it manageable.

For you, a sample library may or may not be important. Find the thing that drives your work and display that. Pull back the curtain on your design inspirations, your thinking, the objects and ideas that make you uniquely you. When your client sees the collection of things that comprise you the designer, they'll undoubtedly have a deeper connection to you. Always remember that people hire people, not images of work.

Each one of the 'essentials' listed above will make your job as a designer or architect easier, but very few are actually required to do the work. If you're invested in making your business a success, you may surprise yourself with how resourceful you become.

You probably have a vision in your head of your ideal studio – we all do. But the reality is that the ideal studio doesn't come before you have the work to support it. It's rational to think the place to start is by creating the perfect work environment and everything else will follow. I hope you're now able to see how that logic is inherently flawed.

Decide what makes you unique in the world and craft your surroundings to tell your story – build your studio around that. That's essential; convey your brand message at every chance. Your studio space is a reflection of you, of your work habits, and of your brand. If you seek clients that match your mission statement and align with the values you project, in time you'll build up a body of work and profitable projects that supports your brand. This is the vehicle that will allow you to create the studio you've always dreamed of. It's not enough to know the steps; you have to take them in the right order to truly make them work.

10 | Startup Costs

"Stop sketching. Start building."
- Dennis Crowley

The day I opened my business was the day that I realized, for the first time in my life I was building my dreams, not someone else's. Think about that, it's emotionally exhilarating isn't it? There are real costs associated with making that happen, some are ones you've probably never considered. How about the cost of not opening your business?

When I was readying to set out on my own, I sought out any resource I could find describing real-world case studies of architects who had gone before me. One in particular stood out in my mind. It was an interview with a founder of a small firm. She ticked off all the boxes you would expect: experience, business savvy, design chops, construction know-how. Then the interviewer asked her what her total start-up costs were, which she happily shared (and I'm paraphrasing here), "Roughly $60,000."

My jaw dropped.

I was deflated. Each expense she recounted was backed by sound logic. But to me, the thought of saving $60,000 to bankroll an unknown business venture not only sounded like a bad idea, it sounded unattainable.

I remembered back to when I financed my home and I was told a similar thing, "You'll need to save at least 20% of the loan value." I was disappointed to hear this, but I knew there had to be a better (less expensive) way. There was. I purchased the land with a construction loan and put just $3,000 down. At the time that was about 1% of the estimated cost to build!

Happily, having successfully opened my business without saving $60,000, I can say that there is another way. In fact, there are many other ways.

If you wait until you're able to save tens of thousands of dollars to do this, it's likely that your dream will never get out of your head and into reality. Money is a perceived barrier to many start-ups, but it's also a chance to be creative and spend it on the 20% of your business that nets you 80% of your revenues.

So what is the other way? It's called "The Lean Start-up." It's described thoroughly in a book by Eric Rees of the same name. The basic premise requires that you build a minimum viable product (MVP) and offer that for sale in the world. The MVP is like a rough sketch of your business. It doesn't have all the bells and whistles of an established one, but it's enough to begin earning revenues. It's a working proof of concept that requires a minimal investment to initiate. You'll figure out what works along the way and make changes all without sinking a lot of money into ideas or accouterments you don't need.

The lean start-up methodology is the path I think you should take because it looks for ways to avoid spending cash on things that aren't important. It allows you to focus on getting the work and doing the work not on building things you don't need – like a new studio.

You'll still have to invest some money in a few important items. So how much will starting up your firm cost? A lot less than $60,000.

Business Structure. In Chapter 2 we outlined various business structures. A sole proprietorship or partnership costs nothing to create, even a limited liability company (LLC) is inexpensive to establish. Here in Maine, where I practice, it's about $200 to file the applications. If that's too intimidating, services like LegalZoom can help you organize all the paperwork for $99 plus your state filing fee. These filing fees vary based on the state you'll be operating in; Illinois is the highest at $612 in Illinois while Arkansas is the lowest at $45. Corporations are yet more expensive. Lean start-ups will choose either the LLC, sole proprietorship, or a partnership.

Cost:
Sole proprietorship or partnership: $0
LLC: $150 +/- (State dependent)

Licenses and permits. This is another category where the fees are regulated by the individual state. If your state requires that you maintain a license to practice the kind of work you do you'll need to contact the state licensing board to determine the costs involved. In Maine, my architecture license costs $75 per year, but some states charge in the hundreds of dollars. To maintain my professional record with the National Council of Architectural Registration Boards I submit an annual fee of $225. The NCARB council record allows architects to apply for reciprocity (for an additional fee) in other states. This keeps the door open for me to work in different regions of the United States. On a local level, I filed a Doing Business As form along with a $10 fee when I opened my business. Check with your town or city to determine their requirements.

Cost: From $300 to $700 depending on your state and local fees.

Professional Liability (PL) Insurance. In some parts of the world, professional liability insurance is mandatory. Be sure to check with the local authorities because insurance costs will count among your biggest expenditures if it's compulsory. Insurance costs can vary greatly depending on your experience level, the coverage you select, your exposure to risk and the deductible. Some variables will be unknowable to you, things like your annual billings and net revenues.

The high cost of this insurance often deters new business owners from purchasing it in their first few years. Although it's expensive, getting sued is sure to be even more costly. The design and construction business is fraught with risk. There are large sums of money at stake for your client and for the builder. When you're involved in a project and problems arise, fingers are pointed at the construction pros and the design pros. There's not even a question that you'll assume professional responsibility for your work, it's a given. If you're a sole proprietor practicing without PL insurance is especially risky because everything you own could become collateral in a lawsuit. Your assets and the business assets are one and the same. This is a decision with serious consequences. Some argue that you can't afford not to have coverage.

Cost: $0 (higher risk) to $5,000+ per year dependent upon coverage, risk level and deductibles.

Health Insurance. This is now a required cost if you're living in the U.S. Your premium will be based on your age, health, where you live, and your lifestyle. If you have insurance through your current employer, you'll want to continue that coverage until you find a replacement policy. Or, you can opt to pay the penalty when you file your taxes each April.

Cost: Varies.

Branding. Lean start-ups can't afford to outsource graphic design costs for branding, which can run into the tens of thousands for established companies. You're in charge of designing your logo your letterhead and your business cards. Your brand is the asset you're building. Take time early on when you don't have much work on your boards to design your "corporate branding." Do so knowing that you can always pivot as you move forward based on emerging priorities. Understand that your brand *will* change over time; this isn't a final decision. No one is watching yet, you're free to make mistakes that the Coca-Colas of the world aren't.

Cost: $0 (plus sweat equity)

Marketing. Generating new leads and landing projects – business development – is a time-consuming but critical task and it's all your responsibility. You can't afford the tens of thousands of dollars a marketing consultant would cost but you can poach a few of their tricks.

First you need a website, Chapter 4 will get you set up and Chapter 5 will give you insider marketing tips. Your website is the hub of your marketing efforts and your virtual studio. Once that's established, each of your marketing efforts will act as a single spoke that leads back to the center of the hub. There are many free platforms online to being building the spokes; a good place to start is with your Houzz.com profile. It's a vast marketplace with many buyers ready to hire designers for their upcoming projects. There's Facebook, Pinterest, LinkedIn, Instagram, Architizer, and Behance too. Each is an opportunity to build credibility and help you to be discovered in online searches.

Free press, writing online, publishing in magazines, these are all opportunities for free marketing for your business. They also establish professional credibility and hone your writing skills. Guest posting on a blog with a larger audience than you have is great free press. I developed a simple "Design Workshop" for Apartment Therapy and I saw a massive bump in traffic. You can write your own blog, or start a YouTube channel, write for Houzz, or create an e-book around your design specialty.

Of course, marketers use paid ads too, if you could pay a dollar and receive five in return that's a deal you'd do all day long right? Facebook, Pinterest, and Google all have ad programs you can try, but the ROI is difficult to calculate for a design business. When selling products, it's a straightforward exercise to determine the lifetime value of a customer and figure out what you're willing to pay to get one. For service-related businesses it's much harder.

A typical project will net me as little as 10K and as much as 100K. Would I be willing to pay 10% of that fee to secure a client? Perhaps, but does spending $1,000 on Google ads get me that client? I'm not sure. I'd probably invest $1,000 of my own time (a full day of billable time) into developing content for my website before I put any money into paid online ads. Paid online advertising can work, but they require a place for the potential client to arrive at (your website) and it has to be a place that will convince them to take the next step (call you).

Spend time developing the resource first, and then investigate paid ads by hiring a professional to help you do a targeted test run before committing a large marketing budget to paid traffic. Building your organic search traffic will help you honestly evaluate the success of your marketing skills and it's the solution that avoids committing to paying for leads. Building your site into a resource for your potential client takes time; it's a long strategic play (chess) not a quick win (checkers).

Paid print ads are too expensive for your lean business and to work well you must sign on for a long-term run, usually 6 months or more. I prefer the free press strategy to be featured in a magazine article rather than pay for placement.

There are also e-mail lists, direct mail marketing, and reaching out to your network – you'll run out of time long before your free options have expired.

Cost: $0 (plus sweat equity)

Website. Purchase a domain for your business in .com (.net, .biz) form, a theme for your site, and a hosting company. Building your site and crafting your brand message has never been more affordable. Houzz.com offers free web hosting and website templates. They make it easy to set up, automatically populating it with your profile information and the projects you've uploaded to Houzz. However, I strongly recommend against using it. This is your business, you want to control the assets, not sublet them to another large corporation. Houzz is better at SEO than you. If you hand over every asset you have to them, they may outrank you in local search for your own business. Besides, if they pivot in a direction you don't agree with, or dissolve, what happens to your assets? They go too.

Having your own website means you can build the spokes back to your property, not theirs. Domains (.com, .net, .biz) are a form of online real estate and there's a finite number of catchy names, claim yours now and start building.

Cost: $150 +/- for a domain, your theme and an annual hosting plan.

Studio. The lean start-up will begin by working from home. What your working environment looks like has little to do with the success of your business. Invest your time into finding work and landing projects not a posh studio. This will give you a longer runway, time for the business to build a local foothold and you'll have the freedom to choose projects based on fit not cash flow. You can still make your home studio reflective of your brand's message by curating what's displayed and offering a peek at your design process and the tools you use to design.

Cost: $0. Your rent or mortgage and living expenses remain a direct cost to you, so it's not truly free. However, if you claim the Home Office Deduction part of those living expenses can be used to offset your tax liabilities.

Furniture. You'll need a few essentials to get started: a worktable, a meeting table, a light, bookcases, a filing cabinet, and a couple of chairs.

Cost: $450 +/-. Use existing furniture or ply local tag sales and flea markets for something interesting. There's always IKEA too.

Office supplies. Pens, pencils, trace, paper, binders, file folders, sketchpads – you'll need an assortment of each. You probably already have much of this lying in wait.

Cost: $100

Smart phone. Your mobile office, camera, phone, and office assistant rolled into one. Although it doesn't fit neatly with the lean start-up model, I think it's an essential tool. Keep track of the business use of your phone, come tax time you'll need to assign a percentage to it in order to calculate your deduction. I think 90% is a reasonable starting point, but yours will vary.

Cost: $300 for phone, $100 for monthly service.

Internet and Phone (landline). Separating your business and personal life is not only good business practice; it's an important part of maintaining your own sanity and health. The IRS doesn't allow you to deduct the cost of your home's primary landline but it does allow the cost of a second line used for business. Having a dedicated business line and voice-mail neatly compartmentalizes this aspect of your business. If possible, bundle your phone service with your Internet service (another essential) to reap additional savings.

Cost: $100 +/- per month.

Computer hardware and Equipment. Repurpose an existing laptop or desktop system if possible. If that's not an option, plan to purchase a midlevel laptop. This can serve as a mobile office when you need to get away from home, a presentation tool for client meetings, and a production workstation. When selecting a system consider the drawing software you'll be using, not all CAD programs are available on both Mac and PC platforms.

Cost: $0 - $2,500.

Software. There are a few types of software you'll need to get started.

Drawing software has such a wide range of pricing structures it's hard to be specific without knowing the exact package you'll be using. Free options abound, but verify they're compatible with the rest of the world (and your consultants). You'll also need to consider the cost of the time it takes to learn how to use it and time when you're not producing at full capacity. If saving $5,000 in software costs means you'll spend 500 hours learning it, that's a bad trade. As a business owner, you should always be thinking about the entire picture before making a decision.

Cost:
Basic Entry Level CAD: $0
Upgraded: $1,000
Basic BIM (Building Information Modeling): $1,500 – $2,000
Full BIM: $5,000+

See Chapter 12 for more on choosing drawing, modeling and graphical presentation software.

Word Processing, presentation and spreadsheet tools can be had for free by using Google Docs with a Gmail account. Microsoft Office is relatively inexpensive at $220. Evernote (or OneNote) is another free option, which I use to catalog meeting notes and other project information in an eminently searchable database. Sign-up for free cloud storage on Dropbox and keep all your files there. This saves you from having to purchase a separate backup drive and storage system.

Cost: $0 – $220.

Accounting and bookkeeping must be done, but as a lean start-up you'll be doing it. It's intimidating at first, but you'll need to develop these skills to run a profitable business you can't farm them out yet. I prefer the cloud-based accounting programs that automatically integrate with my business bank account and offer streamlined payment and invoicing. Companies like: QuickBooks online, Harvest, Xero, Freshbooks or Wave (free) are great options. The industry standard is QuickBooks, but I found it wasn't easy to use.

Working billable time will require time tracking software too if it's not integrated into your software already. There are many free online tools; my personal favorite is Toggl whose tagline is, "insanely simple time tracking."

Cost:
Cloud-based free: $0
Cloud-based subscription: $10 - 30 +/- per month
QuickBooks: $200 (plus time learning)

Integrated project management software packages all the above functions into one program. ArchiOffice is a good example of a solution developed by architects for architects, which handles time tracking, invoicing, and a project inventory. It's useful for larger offices and project teams and is worthy of consideration if your plans including scaling your business. Having used ArchiOffice before, I found it to be feature-rich, but equally bug-laden, not entirely intuitive and it had a substantial learning curve. Campfire, Basecamp and other paid options abound. Trello and Asana are excellent free options you can test to get a feel for how good project management software can help you organize tasks.

Cost:
$0 (free or not necessary for a sole proprietor)
$20 month (billed annually)

Printer, copier, scanner. I recommend going all digital. Convince your clients to go paperless by showing them everything in digital format. Catalogue all of your documents this way too. There's really no need for hard copies if everything is digitally searchable and backed up. It's likely that at some point you'll still need to do some printing and scanning. Check the cost of consumables like ink or toner before purchasing.

Cost:
All digital: $0
Inkjet, laser printer, scanner: $150 - $200

Plotter. Having a large format printer in house is convenient but it's not a necessity. You can make this purchase when you secure your first paying project; that's what I did. If you have access to reprographic services locally, this purchase can wait a long time. If you'll be making regular use of a repro service be sure to include the cost of prints in your contract as a recoverable reimbursable expense, they add up quickly.

When you do decide to purchase a plotter, as above, consider the cost of consumables, size, and output limitations before finalizing your decision. You can spend a large sum on a plotter, but there's little need to, a good basic inkjet from HP will serve you well for many years. If you need upgraded resolutions, special media and higher output quality you can farm it out to a shop with a better plotter and recoup the cost of the prints from your client.

Cost: $0 for third-party repro services; $1000 + for a plotter.

As you purchase these items, keep track of the expenses in your accounting software. For tax purposes things like office equipment, computers, software, and furniture are subject to depreciation. Each durable good you own has a specific life span according to the IRS. Essentially, they assume that the purchase of equipment for use in your business has a useable life which exceeds a year – a computer, for example. When that's the case you divide the value of the equipment over its useable lifespan and that's the deduction you're allowed in a single tax year.

An important exception to this rule is described in Section 179 of the tax code, which says you can write-off the full value of the equipment in a single year. For 2015, these Section 179 deductions are capped at $25,000. This cap has been increased to $500,000 consistently by Congress during the year, but it resets to $25,000 every January 1st.

Professional advice. When starting your business you'll need to rely on the collective wisdom of those who have gone before you and those with more experience than you. This is especially true for aspects of your business that expose your personal assets to risk. Seeking professional advice for contract language, accounting and bookkeeping, and your business structure will often save you far more than your initial investment. You'll have enough to contend with just securing and doing the work without the added stress of formulating a tax strategy and protecting your personal assets. Not doing so is the equivalent of your client thinking they can design their own home or interiors to save money.

If possible, try to cultivate at least one or two other professional mentorships to help with your business. These relationships don't necessarily have to be in your field. All small-business owners have similar concerns and having the counsel of someone who has done this before and access to their network is invaluable especially when the inevitable unfamiliar situation arises.

Cost:
$0 for professional mentorship;
$150 - $500+ for lawyer, financial adviser, accounting advice.

The final cost is one you'll have to confront whether or not you decide to start your own business.

Opportunity cost. Given two mutually exclusive options – working for someone else or choosing to work for you – the opportunity cost is the value not enjoyed if you were to choose the next-best option. Starting a business isn't for everyone, but if you've always dreamed of doing so you should evaluate exactly what you're trading by not pursuing it. These costs are substantial and each day you defer your dream is a day that you're not building your asset, your contacts, your network, your reputation and offering the unique skill-set only you can bring to your future clients.

It's up to you to take action, to make the leap and take that difficult first step. Don't continue to build someone else's dream by sacrificing yours. If the business doesn't turn out to be the success you're imagining, you'll still have the life experience of building a business. Personally, that's something I'd never trade. Starting my business has provided opportunities I never would have imagined when I was an employee working to build someone else's dream.

Total Cost. I've tried to make this list as exhaustive as possible but within it there's lots of flexibility. In reality, there are only four physical things you need to start a design business: a phone, a place to work, a laptop and a website. If you don't already own a laptop the sum total to open your business requires around $4,000 to get started, closer to $1,500 if you can repurpose one you already own.

That's a raw cost and it doesn't include any savings you'll need to live on while you secure commissions. Retool your personal budget to align with the lean start-up model and your savings will provide and even longer runway.

Starting your own business won't be like anything you've done before. You won't draw a paycheck every two weeks and you'll have to adopt a new attitude toward budgeting and distinguishing between needs and wants. You're signing up for at least a few initial, lean years, and if that thought combined with an investment of a couple of thousand dollars seems too risky or unpleasant then you're not ready yet.

The return on your investment is difficult to quantify. After all, your brand has never existed in the world. What value can it bring to your clients, to the built environment, your family, your own life? These intangibles are impossible to assign a dollar value to.

The mental challenges of opening your business eclipse the physical necessities. You'll need thick skin; determination, commitment, dedication, and a strong resolve to work through the problems you'll face. If you wait for all the lights to be green to make the leap, you'll never do it. The mental foundations won't cost you a thing, there's no saving to do, no shipping costs, no assembly. Take the first step today toward opening your own business – you'll be glad you did.

11 | SOP's

"We are what we repeatedly do." - Aristotle

As a designer, you have a natural affinity for systems – structural, mechanical, ordering – you rely on these to organize your design work and your business will benefit from applying this rational approach too. In time, you'll settle into a comfortable routine in your business. But, it's easy to confuse routines with systems, and routines don't always correlate with the best (or expected) outcomes. This is why having a set of standard operating procedure (SOP) documents makes good business sense.

SOP documents precisely define the set of steps necessary to complete a task given a specific cue - a new client inquiry, for example. Each SOP document ensures you're following a predetermined set of steps required to produce an optimal result. Leads will enter your marketing funnel where you'll convert them into clients, then do the work and deliver the intended product. How seamlessly this happens is up to you and systems ensure you don't miss any details along the way.

The first step toward developing your SOP documents is to write down your mission statement. Keep it brief, one page at most, and speak honestly about what your brand is and the change it's seeking to effect in the world. Your SOP documents should be crafted to support this mission statement. Refer to it as if it were a design concept even as you develop the mundane procedures.

Communication SOP. Good communication is crucial to the success of any professional. If you're good at it, communication can be a strong differentiator, one that matters to clients. The construction industry is notorious for poor communication. The goal of your communication SOP should be timely, open, and transparent communication always. Begin by asking your client how they prefer to communicate: Skype, text, e-mail, or phone. I like to check in with clients regularly (once a week or so) during the design process to keep them informed about progress and engaged in the process.

Engaged clients are much less likely to be surprised by a large invoice because they know the care you've been investing in their project throughout the month. They also tend to value your counsel more. Although you're well aware of the time it takes to design between the thinking, the drawing, and the redrawing; your client isn't unless you show them. If all they see is a polished sketch at the end of a week's worth of work, they'll have a harder time reconciling the $3,000 bill for the time it took to get there.

Open communication allows the process behind the sketch to be revealed to the client and they can better appreciate the complexities, iterative nature and struggles latent in the design process. The better they understand this the easier it is to correlate process with price and value. The way I look at it is this, my client is paying me to sketch, I might as well show them the bad ideas along with the good. One other benefit to doing this is that the bad ideas have special power to reinforce the good ones.

Communicating schedule changes should be an important part of your SOP too. Dragging out a schedule can impact your bottom line and your client's too. Hourly work that drags on means the client will pay more, while fixed fee projects will impact your profitability. Be honest when things aren't going the way everyone planned, it's the only fair thing to do. You'll build a reputation for being forthright among your clients and professional contacts which is invaluable in the business world.

Systems. All this communicating takes time and if you're going to do it efficiently you'll need systems in place to speed the process and allow you to deliver a consistent message each and every time. The mechanics of these systems are usually templates or forms that you can pull and quickly personalize and send without having to think about them.

For example, there will be a steady stream of inquiries from prospective clients entering your marketing funnel via your website. If you don't develop a system for responding to these inquiries, you'll spend a lot of time answering the same questions repeatedly.

We discussed a few ways to handle this situation in Chapter 5; here they are again. Direct any inquires to a prepopulated marketing page where they answer questions you've developed to prescreen them. Ask the questions that will help you decide whether you're a good fit before they even contact you (style, budget, schedule, scope, type, etc.) This saves time for you and them. By the time the initial phone call happens, you'll already know they're a good fit based on their answers to your questions. And you won't waste time discussing project you'll already know the details and can move on to the next step together. This also starts to get a client invested in a process – your process – and will mean they're more likely to want to work with you.

Another option is to develop an e-mail template with a link in it directing them to a frequently asked questions (FAQ) page. Populate the FAQ with all the questions you receive every time you speak with a client – schedule, cost, program, etc. As new questions come in, answer them once on the FAQ page and you'll always have an updated reference to direct inquiring clients to.

By learning to think in systems, you'll find many ways to use your time more wisely. As a bonus these systems are symbiotic, they help your client and your business to use time efficiently. The client doesn't have to waste time e-mailing or calling to figure out whether your business is best positioned to help them. Equally, you don't have to spend time answering the same questions again and again wondering if you're delivering the same or slightly different messaging each time.

If you make only one SOP, make it your communication SOP.

What works for me: My basic framework for communication is to respond to everything I receive (aside from spam). My brand touts collaboration as its selling point and there's no better way to underscore that brand message than by responding to people when they contact me. This includes salespeople, contractors, clients, potential clients, students – anyone.

Having systems in place to do that efficiently enables me to do this. I have a resource of prepopulated templates for responses to nearly every question I've been asked. Most popular are the new client inquiries and process oriented questions. On-boarding new clients can be time-consuming but when a new project is worth $10,000 – $100,000 to my business, time spent making the experience easier and more open pays big dividends. I've committed to a maximum response time for all correspondence from clients and prospective clients of 24 hours without exception. Many times the response is, "I received your message and I'm working on a solution. I'll be in touch shortly." As problems inevitably arise during the design and construction process, open communication engenders understanding, if not always happy clients.

Project Management. Paper to-do lists might be your thing, but going pro will demand a more integrated solution. There are many apps and software available for project management. Some are tailored specifically to the AEC industry like ArchiOffice; others are more general and handle only basic task management. Michael Kilkelly, a practicing architect, developed an excellent flow-chart to help you decide the best fit for your needs (archsmarter.com/project-management-software). Do you need to manage teams? Do you need integrated invoicing and time tracking? Do you need Gmail integration?

At a minimum you'll need a means of tracking time for billing, accounting software for financial housekeeping, task and project information management, and contact management. With teams, it becomes more crucial to integrate these solutions in one place. As an individual, you have more freedom to experiment with a variety of solutions.

Lean start-ups will choose from one of the many free applications to handle time tracking, project management and invoicing. Invest some time researching the options and pick one or two to start using. Keep it simple. You'll quickly find what works and what doesn't and pivot if you need to.

As you build your team and scale your practice (assuming that's your goal), project management will take on a different meaning. You'll have to decide how you'll orchestrate the delivery of the work you've always done yourself. Project management won't be strictly related to project delivery, it will extend to compensating employees, tracking their time for invoicing, managing benefits and vacation time and making payroll. The more integrated solutions handle this better, but they're harder to learn and more expensive.

Time tracking. Even if you're working on a fixed fee, you should track the time you spend on projects as a reference for future proposals. Tracking it for hourly work is essential. If you've opted for project management software, this is probably built-in. I can say from experience having cobbled together various systems in my practice, integrated solutions are admirably convenient. However, without that option you'll need to track your billable time separately. You can use Excel, Google Docs, or Evernote. Or use one of the thousands of software solutions available for download or in the cloud.

What works for me: I use a combination of software to manage my projects. Project Task Management: Asana (cloud based, free). Project Master Files: Dropbox. Time tracking: Toggl (cloud based, free). Fee tracking: Excel. Accounting/Invoicing: Wave Accounting (cloud based, free) Contacts: on my phone backed up to iCloud. Everything else: Evernote.

Procedures. If you don't opt for an all-inclusive software solution for project management, it's important to have a framework or system in place to use when you begin a new project. Storing and syncing your data to the cloud is the most reliable and redundant option available. Sign up for an account with Dropbox, Box, or Carbonite, Google Drive or similar cloud storage plan. Most have free plans available with data caps.

Documentation. Phone calls, meeting notes, schedules, drawings, milestones, bid documents, code analyses, field reports and owner provided documents– develop a system for organizing and storing this information for easy retrieval. These tasks are possible to do without project management software but they require a system for doing them the same way each time. The easiest thing to do is correlate the files with each phase of the design work – Predesign, Schematic Design and so forth.

What works for me: I set up a master file in Dropbox for each project. Inside those master files are folders for each phase of the work and separate folders for invoicing and client correspondence. Dropbox allows sharing of these folders with my clients without me having to e-mail them all the information in the folder. When I save meeting notes into a file that I've shared with my client they see the meeting notes.

When I update PDF floor plans, they can see the most recent design.

Doing this contributes to and supports my communication SOP discussed in step one. Sharing also saves the time it would take to draft and send a new e-mail each time I update project relevant information. If there's ever a question about the most current information or set of documents, I always refer the client to the Dropbox folders. After a few times doing this, they learn to look for the information there first and don't have to ask anymore.

Design Schedule. Getting the schedule SOP correct will be difficult early on. Make your best guess and be prepared to be wrong. So long as you're forthcoming with schedule changes and setbacks as they occur, you'll find most clients will be forgiving of a miscalculation. Project complexity, client, scope of work and specific project requirements make this a challenging exercise even for experienced architects and designers. Because of this, I can't offer specific guidelines for setting your schedule.

If you're a sole proprietor responsible for all your business operations, don't assume you'll be able to work the 85-90% billable time you worked as an employee. For scheduling and budgeting purposes, a more realistic guideline is 50%. This means you'll spend the other 50% on business development, answering the phone, e-mail, invoicing, and marketing.

Other systems documents you may consider developing:

> *Programming worksheet, client questionnaire, new project inventory sheet (existing, new), code and zoning checklist, site analysis checklist, meeting notes template, client authorization (to act on their behalf), phase specific checklists (SD, DD, CD), schedule templates (window, door, hardware, lighting, finishes, plumbing include general notes), field report template, budgeting spreadsheet.*

These documents don't necessarily need to be developed ahead of time; compile them as you work on your early projects and save them as master templates for future work.

Another option is to purchase a preformatted library of documents to get you started. If you're looking to save time and implement a system grounded in proven best-practices, I've curated my most useful documents into a package called the

Architect + Entrepreneur Startup Toolkit available for download here: http://thirtybyforty.com/spl. They're the SOPs, fee proposal templates, email templates, business structure, branding resources, client questionnaires, fee tracks cheat-sheets and resources I use daily to run 30X40 Design Workshop.

Marketing. This is a placeholder for you and a reminder that while you're busy delivering the work to your clients and making them happy, you can't neglect your marketing funnel. Make sure you're consistently trying to solicit new leads. If you expend all your energies on project delivery and none on business development, you'll finish out your projects to be left with only empty boards and a gaping hole in your schedule. Even if it seems that the big project you're working on now will never end, it will be over sooner than you think and new leads take time to cultivate and onboard.

Designing the Experience. It's possible to incorporate design into any task you assume. Your business is charged with delivering a specific type of work to your clients. You determine how you'll be compensated, how to protect your personal assets, how to structure your contract, and all the minutiae of delivering the product to them. These are the fundamentals, the foundations, things you must do.

The means – the how – you go about doing them is up to you to design.

Take a step back for a minute to consider the very first time a client comes into contact with your brand. What does that look like? What is the experience? What do you say? You can design that experience – everything from the plates to the napkins. Make it something special, something that complements your brand identity. You could design a menu of services that your client can choose deliverables from – appetizers, entrees, dessert. Include your contract as part of the menu too. Or produce a video or a book. Or not. Be clever and creative.

To continue the menu metaphor, is your menu à la carte; is it a buffet or a chef's tasting menu? There's a strong distinction between full service and limited service business models. Full-service means you'll deliver the entire experience from start to finish. Although this usually ensures the best product possible, it's also a highly exclusive arrangement. You'll have fewer clients to choose from. Along with bigger budgets these clients have higher expectations, and lawyers. You'll do fewer projects but potentially earn more. You can craft a brand around any type of work and your target market will guide your decision as you move forward.

Design the unique experience you want your clients to have. It doesn't have to look like anyone else's firm, your competitors, Bjarke Ingels, or any of the ideas above. Owning your own practice means you make the decisions. There are no committees to consult or consensus to develop or bosses second-guessing you.

Too often when we think about our businesses we forget that we're designers. You have a special set of skills to bring to bear on each and every one of the business decisions you'll face. Your SOPs are a chance to bolster the brand you're crafting in subtle but important ways. Now that you're armed with the fundamentals of running a design business, it's up to you to creatively leverage this business acumen to define the form and shape of your brand.

12 | Software

"I prefer drawing to talking. Drawing is faster, and leaves less room for lies." -Le Corbusier

Design professionals use visuals and drawings as the primary means of communication. The way you compose a set of drawings, the sheet layout and order, the line weights, the notation, the font, shade and shadow, the look and feel of them all contribute to how well they communicate your ideas to the professionals you're relying on to construct the work. Like everything else we've been discussing, they're a part of your brand. Achieving the end result is far more important than the tools you use to get there.

Note: This chapter is dedicated to the specialized software we use as designers and architects. For a more general discussion of office related software, be sure to read Chapter 9, Studio Essentials.

Chances are you're coming to this chapter already with strong preferences about the tools you'll use to do the work. Software is just that, another tool in your toolbox. There are fundamentally two types of software you use to do your professional work which will be the focus of this chapter. drawing and presentation. Let's begin with the foundation of the production side of your business your drawing or CAD (computer-aided design) software.

Few things incite more passionate debate than the selection of CAD software among architects and designers. I'm not here to endorse one program or one methodology over another; just as I wouldn't tell you which pen or which color trace to use (I'm partial to white). Rather this chapter should be used to help you decide which is the right one to use to convey your brand message and help you get the work done.

2D (Drafting) versus 3D (Model Making)

The first choice you'll face is whether to pursue a 2-dimensional or a 3-dimensional, also known as BIM (building information modeling) drawing package. They're completely different means of putting together a drawing set and we're fast moving away from the 2D approaches in favor of the 3D.

Two-dimensional drafting is purely representational, meaning lines only represent 3D objects. These lines in space are in no way interrelated. The drawings don't ever coalesce into a working model of a building. It's up to you to decide which drawings to create and how to draw them based on your knowledge of architectural conventions – the plans, elevations, and sections – that make up a standard drawing set.

Three-dimensional or BIM software by contrast, creates a real, working (and interrelated) model of the building. Drawings are created by slicing and viewing the model in different ways. Need a floor plan? Slice the model at the 4-foot elevation. A section? Slice it vertically at the appropriate location.

The model is imparted with all manner of real-world information. This "intelligent" model allows you to define materials, wall heights, windows, doors, roofs and structure. Each component of the model is a parametric, information-rich object that interacts with the model in very specific ways.

For example, when you insert a window into the plan view of your model you assign it a subset of information: type, size, color, glazing, etc. When the model is viewed from the side you'll see the window has already been drawn at the size you entered and it will have a window tag assigned to it. You can then generate a schedule of the windows you've entered quite quickly.

You'll draw the actual wall construction, the roof planes and the structure. Information can be layered on to the model by your consultants – mechanical, electrical, plumbing – and the systems can achieve a high level of coordination because it's easy to see how they're interrelated in physical space.

The real power of BIM is evidenced when changes are made. It's clear just how much more efficient the 3D drawing environment is compared to the 2D one. Not having to draft static representations – 2D drawings – means less time doing menial tasks and more designing (in theory).

Platform. Other factors influencing your decision will be availability on your computing platform of choice. Not every program has been ported to both Mac and PC operating systems. Autodesk only recently made AutoCAD available for the Mac and it's a different user interface. Don't expect the same experience between the same software on different computers.

Learning curve. To achieve proficiency with any CAD software is a long-term investment, which eclipses the initial or monthly recurring cost. If you're transitioning from 2D to BIM, you might consider an online training course to accelerate your learning.

Depending on how your billing system is structured this can either reward you or pass the spoils of efficiency along to your client. If you work on a fixed fee model, you're always looking for faster ways to do the same amount of work. If you bill hourly, efficiency translates into a lower fee. Either way, time is a fixed resource and it makes sense to always be time-efficient.

There's much to consider and the number of programs available is staggering. There's an excellent Wikipedia entry (en.wikipedia.org/wiki/Comparison_of_computer-aided_design_editors), which compiles many of them into one table for comparison.

Here's a quick review of the basic choices.

2D CAD

The dominant player in the two-dimensional CAD world is Autodesk and their ubiquitous AutoCAD software. They've developed specialized product suites that extend the functionality of AutoCAD. Each suite is aimed at a different design niche and combines a variety of software into one package. Architects and designers are primarily concerned with either AutoCAD or AutoCAD LT and the Building Design software suites. The fully featured AutoCAD distinguishes itself from LT in many ways but primarily it has a more robust set of options, tool palettes, and it's 3D capable. With AutoCAD you also have the option to purchase add-on suites designed specifically for architectural drawing. It's built on a completely different programming language than LT so third-party software options and plug-ins are also more robust. Fundamentally, LT is a stripped-down version of AutoCAD. It's light in every sense of the word and fits the lean start-up model with respect to price and feature set.

As of the writing of this book, purchasing the full version of AutoCAD outright will set you back $4,195. An annual subscription with a basic support plan (which is required) comes in lower at $1,680, while a monthly subscription is $210. Assuming you can afford it, the annual rate will save you $840 a year. With any software investment, you'll need to factor in the upgrade paths too. If you upgrade more frequently than 2 ½ years, the annual subscription model is least expensive while less frequently would steer you toward an outright purchase (if you can afford it).

The light (LT) version is substantially less expensive. To purchase AutoCAD LT will cost $1,380 with an annual subscription cost of $360. If you plan to upgrade more frequently than every 3 ½ years, the annual subscription model is the more cost-efficient choice.

If you're looking for a free tool, Draftsight is comparable in capability to LT and Trimble's SketchUp has an integrated sheet composition tool called LayOut. I found the drafting and drawing production tools in LayOut to be cumbersome and far less intuitive than the modeling tools in the program, but it's a free option to explore.

Two-dimensional CAD, no matter how you dissect it is antiquated. It's essentially digital delineation. You craft a set of stand-alone drawings to represent your design and modify each one along the way as the design inevitably changes. It requires a lot of repetitive, redundant and time-consuming input from you, the user. However, when you've used 2D CAD for any length of time there's an inertia you'll be forced to overcome. You have a set of conventions in place and your drawing sets coalesce without a second thought. Revisions are an accepted part of project delivery process. In this respect, 2D CAD is appealing because it simply gets out of the way.

There's a good chance you'll want 3D capability at some point too; to aid you in the design process and to help your client visualize your ideas. To fill the void you'll have to supplement with (and learn) a 3D program.

Advantages: low initial investment, minimal learning curve, quick means of producing drawings, industry standard file conventions (.dwg, .dxf) allow easy data exchange with consultants.

Disadvantages: revisions require cross coordination among disconnected drawings, drawing set management takes more time, industry standards are moving toward BIM compliant drawings as deliverables, repetitive, tedious drafting tasks are inherent with this method of drawing, and lack of 3D will require other programs to fill that need.

BIM (Building Information Modeling)

It's taken many years for the AEC industry to embrace BIM. Graphisoft developed a rudimentary version of what we call BIM today with the release of ArchiCad in 1984. It bridged the divide between 2D and 3D by creating a working 3D model. This model was then sliced at various points to create the drawing set. Rather than altering a set of disconnected, static drawings, the user modified the model and the drawings automatically updated.

Adopting a BIM strategy is an altogether different way of thinking about design. It's a far more integrated approach to design because it forces you to create an accurate representation of the real-world structure and all its systems along the way.

Chances are you've had the experience of arriving on a jobsite for a weekly project meeting to find a beam in the way of that row of recessed lights that must be centered on the hallway. BIM helps avoid these sorts of hand-to-forehead experiences by forcing coordination to happen in the less costly digital environment rather than on the very costly construction site.

BIM begins and ends with the model of your design. This model is layered with information as you move forward. Your plans, elevations and sections all feed information back and forth to each other. Placing a window in the plan view automatically means it has a head height, a type, a size and glazing type. This information can be as feature rich or as stripped-down as you like. The more data you add, the more you can extract later. This can be in the form of sections or details or in the form of schedules and energy modeling, etc.

The drawing set is created by capturing various views of the information-rich model you've created. Because each sheet is a view of the overall model, when you change any parametric component in the model, the sheet view automatically updates to reflect the change. You can start to appreciate the time savings this represents as projects become more and more complex.

Dominating the BIM software space are: Autodesk's Building Design Suite Premium, which includes Revit ($6,825 to purchase, $340/month, $2,730 annually), Revit LT Suite ($1,675 to purchase, $505 annual subscription), ArchiCad ($4,250) and Vectorworks (starting at $2,595). SketchUp Pro 2015 is BIM compliant ($590) too. Of course, there are countless others.

It's outside the scope of this book to describe the nuances of each program and technology, pricing, and feature sets change too often to make it a relevant exercise. Search online for reviews and read the opinions of others. Given the difference in price and capabilities among the options it pays to do your research. Up-front cost savings may conceal a far less efficient workflow or minimal feature set. Revit LT, for example, lacks some useful tools – energy and structural analysis – and limits the number of people able to work on a model simultaneously. So while one solution may provide the sole practitioner with entry-level BIM it may be unworkable for a firm intending to scale their workforce and use project teams to complete drawing tasks.

Advantages: realistic representation of the real-world structure, built-in 3D modeling to use for client visualization, rendering and design, saves time on repetitive drawing tasks, real-time coordination of building systems (M/E/P, structural, etc.), competitive advantage in markets requiring BIM as a deliverable.

Disadvantages: high initial cost to purchase, high cost to learn, longer up-front drafting time to create the parametric model, still requires 2D drafting for certain detailed tasks, and plug-ins may be required to create presentable drawing output (Bluebeam).

The more time-intensive, initial modeling tasks can net savings on the back end as changes are made and drawings are updated and automatically cross-coordinated. To be able to mine the data represented in a working 3D model of your structure is invaluable. As we move closer to the future where construction is done with giant 3D printers and drones (perhaps not all that far off) BIM will only become more relevant. The days of 2D drawing are numbered.

How to choose? This decision represents a substantial investment for your business both short and long-term. When you're just getting started you'll never be better positioned to make it. Once you have employees, established conventions, and working projects the inertia will be far greater; perhaps insurmountable. A firm of one (or a few) is nimble enough to test drive anything. Use your low overhead to experiment and pivot as necessary.

Although there's much debate in professional circles about the right approach, I think the choice today is quite easy. If you're not already using a 2D solution (bought and paid for), I would opt for a BIM platform and build your practice around that. If your plans include scaling beyond just you or you and a partner, choose one that will accommodate the aspiration. Your future employees are all being trained to use BIM, you may as well leverage this reality.

If, however, you've been using 2D CAD for your drawings the decision isn't as straightforward. There's a baked in efficiency to plowing ahead with what you know. But when your business is young you may have more free time than you'd like. This is time you can invest in learning new BIM software. As you build your solo practice you'll need to focus on project delivery (and marketing, and billing, and client meetings) not learning on the job.

Conversely, to saddle yourself with another unfamiliar task among all the other new things you'll be juggling will only make the downtime learning more expensive. You need billable time to keep the lights on and if you're frustrated trying to do the tasks you were accustomed to doing without a second thought the runway you've worked so diligently to construct can quickly disappear.

Relying on familiar systems (2D or otherwise), ones that work, can actually be a sensible choice. Software, CAD in particular, is just another tool. If it's not helping produce the work you want your brand to be known for, then something's wrong. Use the tools that produce results for you. Fighting with a CAD program will sap your creativity faster than almost anything else - hand draft if you have to.

In our global economy outsourcing the work is an option too. Hire someone else in-house or remotely to produce your BIM model and drawings. If there's something keeping you from doing your best work, stop and pivot – you're the CEO, you're paid to make strategic decisions.

Presentation Software

With your CAD software decision out of the way, the choices become easier. Even if you opt for 3D CAD, you'll probably need a way to refine and post-process the models and drawings you produce. Modeling, rendering and presentation software makes this possible.

SketchUp is a free, extremely intuitive, modeling program that all architects and designers should learn. The upgraded Pro version is a reasonable outlay at $590 and comes with a more robust feature set. It also allows you to import your CAD files in .dwg and .dxf format. However, either version can be used in 2D, 3D, and BIM configurations and the richness it adds to the design process is unparalleled. The learning curve is virtually nonexistent, it's that intuitive.

The output directly from SketchUp is limited, though; sketchy is a good descriptor. Any of the basic shade and shadowed black-and-white outputs is respectable for projecting a basic sense of a given design, but if you're trying to simulate realistic materials the program falls flat. I often use exported 'renderings' as under-lays for hand sketching, adding materials and details on the basic forms.

To output high-quality, ray traced images from SketchUp you'll want to purchase a third-party application or plug-in. I use the Maxwell for SketchUp plug-in ($99), essentially a rendering engine that sits inside SketchUp and allows you to assign materials to your model and create photo-realistic renderings. Other options are V-ray ($750) and Podium ($198). The downside is most third-party rendering tools aren't nearly as easy to learn as SketchUp.

Heavy-duty rendering software is a significant price jump. Programs like 3D Studio Max ($3,675), Maya ($3,675), Form-Z ($1,390) or Rhino ($1,295) may be worth considering if your workflows are built around higher-level modeling and rendering tasks. Along with their hefty price tags, come steep learning curves. For a small practice, they're probably more horsepower than you need. If you're already well versed in using the software and can bypass the learning stage, they can quickly pay for themselves in time and money saved outsourcing the work. You're also guaranteed to be happy with the results. Offering freelance modeling and rendering services can actually be a separate revenue stream in lean times too.

Photoshop, InDesign, Illustrator
Available by subscription these programs are essential at various points in the design process for layout, compositing and client presentations. The Adobe products are only available via their Creative Cloud subscription model. As a business owner, you'll pay $30 per month (per user) to use any one application. If you need access to all their applications it's $70 per month (per user).

I like the a-la-cart pricing model; it fits with the lean start-up structure we've been following. Buy what you need, when you need it. If you're not sure which is better, Adobe offers free trials of all their products, try each and see which will allow you to deliver a better, finished product and invest your business dollars there.

There are free options available like the open-source Inkscape and GIMP but they feel clunky and consumer-grade compared to Photoshop. Pixlr by Autodesk is free. The closest low-cost alternative Photoshop clone is Pixelmator ($30) but it's only available for the Mac.

Hand Drawing
Even though the drafting table is a relic of a bygone age and pixels have replaced graphite, there's a reason drawing by hand persists – architects and designers draw. Our ability to convey meaning by sketching our ideas lies at the heart of what we do. There is no more powerful tool than the ability to sketch.

The gifted Carlo Scarpa taught a design studio course at the IUAV School of Architecture in Venice where the very first lesson began with the art of sharpening a pencil. From the pencil great architecture follows. The possibility pregnant in the sketch yields a design vision far beyond the page. Sketching is a skill that will serve you throughout your career and pencils don't require upgrades.

What works for me: My production work is done in AutoCAD LT 2015, which I run on both a Mac and a PC (they're actually quite different). I can produce a set of drawings very quickly; I don't think about how to draw, I just draw. It's the same as picking up a pencil for me. However, I will pivot to BIM at the next opportunity, when my workload eases. I use SketchUp Pro for basic modeling tasks along with the Maxwell for SketchUp plug-in for rendering. I use 3D Studio Max on an as-needed subscription basis for higher power modeling and rendering tasks as they come along. However, that's only because I'm familiar with the UI and workflow. If I need images of higher quality than I can produce with those tools, or if I don't have the time, I simply farm it out to one of many 3D service bureaus in Asia. For presentation software, I was fortunate to have purchased Photoshop and Illustrator before they moved to the current cloud-based subscription model.

For hand drawing I use: Pilot Precise V7 (black and red), Pentel Sign pens (black and gray), 5MM / 7MM HB mechanical lead pencils, and Sharpie Ultra Fine Point (black and red). Media varies but it's primarily white trace or Strathmore (of varying weights) in sketchbooks. Muji makes a wonderful array of inexpensive sketchbooks that I really like. For color, I have a set of Prismacolor colored pencils for paper and a collection of 30 or so of their double tipped markers for trace.

Closing Thoughts +

Resources

"If you wait for all the lights to turn green before starting your journey, you'll never leave the driveway." - Zig Ziglar

I'll be honest - I like as many green lights as possible. Architects and design professionals are, by nature, planners. But as anyone who has completed at least a few construction projects knows the process is an organic one with many unplanned events along the way. Your goal is to try to control as many aspects as possible, but more importantly to have a plan in place to respond to those unforeseen events as they occur and move past them.

If you've been following along and taking action on the step-by-step journey to designing your practice, I offer you my sincere congratulations. If you're still contemplating, reading, researching and waffling; I would encourage you to commit to action (one way or another), set aside the fear and give it a try.

Try to honestly answer the question, "What's the worst thing that can happen?" You may find that the 'worst-case scenario' is actually finding another job. It may be a job that's even better than the one you have now.

If you've chosen to open your practice, you have many facets of your business competing for attention. Short-range, weekly focus will be brought to bear on day-to-day operations, getting the work done, speaking with leads, drawing, specifying, marketing, coordinating, and communicating. Your long-range focus, although it demands less overt attention, actually requires more. It has to be directed toward building the asset. I've touched on this throughout the book; your brand is the public face of that asset. You're in control of that as the founder and CEO. It's critical that you have your brand narrative in place to guide your decision-making processes at all the waypoints.

That's something that's yours, which no one can take from you. You'll be charting the course, making the decisions, deciding whether to take a two-hour lunch or to meet with a client on a Sunday morning, or going to the planning board meeting instead of your child's concert.

If your business is to achieve long-term success, you'll need to consistently revisit the themes of the marketing, getting hired and client experience chapters. When you make it through the first eighteen months special recognition is in order. That's a hurdle 80% of new businesses don't clear.

Starting an architecture firm requires more than just ticking boxes on a checklist. It's a life-changing event, and another member of your family, as such it requires constant care and feeding.

You've read about what works for me, you know what to expect and now it's your turn. There's no longer one model of design practice; you're free to create your own. Embrace failure as an integral part of your process and as you pivot and try new things you'll find the intersections of your talents and the world's needs; that's where you'll find your business.

I wish you nothing but success.

Additional Resources

If you'd like access to the resource page compiled exclusively for readers of this book simply enter your email address at: http://thirtybyforty.com/sign-up

Download the tools and resources I use to run 30X40 Design Workshop in the A+E Startup Toolkit Volume 1 located here: http://thirtybyforty.com/spl

Brand Tools
Naming Guide Resource (PDF)
Branding Resource + Links (PDF)
Business Card Template (Images, PSD)
Sample logo (PSD, JPG) + Social Media Icon Pack - B&W (PNGs)

Organizational Tools
Business Structure Cheat Sheet (PDF)
Revenue Model Guide (PDF)
Passive Income Cheat Sheet (PDF)

Email Marketing Tools
Email Capture Resources (PDF)
(15) Email response templates (Word)

Process Tools + Documents
New Client Design Process Guide (Word)
New Client Standard Operating Procedure (SOP) – (Word)
New Client Interview Questions (Word)
Draft Fee Proposal (Word)
New Client Welcome Checklist (Word)
New Client Programming Worksheet - (Excel)
New Client Questionnaire (PDF, Word)
Client Authorization Letter (Word)
Project Fee Tracking Worksheet - (Excel)
Shop Drawing Stamp (PDF, PSD)
General Project Information Document (Word)
Meeting Notes Document (Word)

About the Author

Eric Reinholdt is an award-winning architect, mountain climber, designer, guitar player, paper cutter, blogger and author. He is the founder of 30X40 Design Workshop, a residential design studio bordering Acadia National Park on Mount Desert Island just off the coast of Maine. This is where he lives and practices in a modern Longhouse, with his wife, two boys and one cat.

His architecture is simple, modern, site-specific, and craft-driven. It features local materials and familiar forms juxtaposed against modern, open floor plans with minimalist detailing. The work celebrates humble materials, subtle contrasts and finely crafted details.

Eric is also a curator for Section Cut and a professional weekly contributor for Houzz.com and has authored more than 60 Ideabooks published on their homepage and in newsletters to date.

<u>Connect with Eric:</u>

eric@thirtybyforty.com

Twitter: @EricReinholdt

Instagram: ereinholdt

Facebook: /30x40DesignWorkshop

Printed in Great Britain
by Amazon.co.uk, Ltd.,
Marston Gate.